Collins

PRACTICE MULTIPLE CHOICE QUESTIONS

CSEC®
Physics

Peter DeFreitas

HarperCollins Publishers Ltd
The News Building
1 London Bridge Street
London SE1 9GF

First edition 2017

10 9 8 7 6 5 4 3

ISBN 978-0-00-820087-9

www.collins.co.uk/caribbeanschools

A catalogue record for this book is available from the British Library.

Typeset by QBS Learning
Printed and bound by Grafica Veneta S. P.A.

Author: Peter DeFreitas
Publisher: Elaine Higgleton
Commissioning Editor: Ben Gardiner
Managing Editor: Sarah Thomas
Project Manager: Alissa McWhinnie
Copy Editor: Jane Roth
Proofreader: Aidan Gill
Artwork: QBS Learning
Cover design: Kevin Robbins and Gordon MacGilp
Production: Lauren Crisp

MIX
Paper from responsible sources

FSC™ C007454

FSC™ is a non-profit international organisation established to promote the responsible management of the world's forests. Products carrying the FSC label are independently certified to assure consumers that they come from forests that are managed to meet the social, economic and ecological needs of present and future generations, and other controlled sources.

Find out more about HarperCollins and the environment at
www.harpercollins.co.uk/green

Contents

Download answers free at www.collins.co.uk/caribbeanschools

Introduction

Structure of the CSEC® Physics Paper 1 Examination

There are **60 questions**, known as items, in the Paper 1 examination and the duration of the examination is **1¼ hours**. The paper is worth **30%** of your final examination mark.

The number of questions tested within each section is not fixed. The following table shows an analysis of the approximate number of questions expected within each section.

Section	*Approximate* number of questions
A: Mechanics	18
B: Thermal Physics and Kinetic Theory	9
C: Waves and Optics	9
D: Electricity and Magnetism	17
E: The Physics of the Atom	7
Total	**60**

The questions test two profiles, **knowledge and comprehension**, and **use of knowledge**. Questions will be presented in a variety of ways, including the use of diagrams, data, graphs, prose or other stimulus material.

Each question is allocated 1 mark. You will *not* lose a mark if a question is answered incorrectly.

Examination tips

General strategies for answering multiple choice questions:

- Read every word of each question very carefully and make sure you understand exactly what it is asking. Even if you think that the question appears simple or straightforward, there may be important information you could easily omit, especially small but very important words such as *all* or *only*.

- When faced with a question that seems unfamiliar, re-read it very carefully. Underline or circle the key pieces of information provided. Re-read it again if necessary to make sure you are very clear as to what it is asking and that you are not misinterpreting it.

- Each question has four options, **A**, **B**, **C** and **D**, and only one is the correct answer. Look at all the options very carefully, because the differences between them may be very subtle; never stop when you come across an option you think is the one required. Cross out options that you know are incorrect for certain. There may be two options that appear very similar; identify the difference between the two so you can select the correct answer.

- You have approximately 1¼ minutes per question. Some questions can be answered in less than 1 minute, while other questions may require longer because of the reasoning or calculation involved. Do not spend too long on any one question.

- If a question appears difficult place a mark, such as an asterix, on your answer sheet alongside the question number and return to it when you have finished answering all the other questions.

- Answer every question. Marks are not deducted for incorrect answers. Therefore, it is in your best interest to make an educated guess in instances where you do not know the answer. Never leave a question unanswered.

- Always ensure that you are shading the correct question number on your answer sheet. It is very easy to make a mistake, especially if you skip questions and plan to return to them.

- Some questions may ask which of the options is NOT correct or is INCORRECT. Pay close attention to this because it is easy to fail to see the words 'NOT' or 'INCORRECT' and answer the question incorrectly.

- Some questions may give two or more answers that could be correct and you are asked to determine which is the BEST or MOST LIKELY. You must consider each answer very carefully before making your choice because the differences between them may be very subtle.

- When a question gives three or four answers numbered **I**, **II** and **III** or **I**, **II**, **III** and **IV**, one or more of these answers may be correct. You will then be given four combinations as options, for example:

  (A) I only

  (B) I and II only

  (C) II and III only

  (D) I, II and III

  Place a tick by all the answers that you think are correct before you decide on the final correct combination.

- Do not make any assumptions about your choice of options; just because two answers in succession have been C, it does not mean that the next one cannot be C as well.

- Try to leave time at the end of the examination to check over your answers, but never change an answer until you have thought about it again very carefully.

Strategies for the CSEC® Physics Paper 1:

- Silent, non-programmable calculators are allowed in the examination. Since the different brands of calculator have different methods of accessing the functions it is advisable to use one that you are familiar with.

- Re-check your calculations, because it is quite easy to press the wrong key on the calculator.

- Always examine how reasonable your calculated values are. For example, an adult of mass 5 g would not be possible.

- For numerical answers, ensure that you have considered the prefix to the unit. You may have calculated a value of 0.5 kg but the answer may be represented as 500 g.

- Know how to convert certain units such as those involving areas and volumes. For example, 2 mm^2 is 2×10^{-6} m^2 and *not* 4 mm^2 or 4×10^{-6} m^2 or 2×10^{-9} m^2.

- It is often useful to sketch diagrams. This is particularly important where the effect of several forces is needed to formulate an equation.

- You must know all of the required formulas, definitions, laws and facts. Have these memorised long before the examination so that they will be firmly installed in your memory.

1 The professor who first implemented a scientific approach in order to investigate a problem, and who is often referred to as 'the father of scientific methodology', is

(A) Galileo   Ⓐ

(B) Democritus   Ⓑ

(C) Newton   Ⓒ

(D) Einstein   Ⓓ

2 The bob of a simple pendulum makes 20 complete swings in 40 seconds. Which of the following correctly states the period and frequency of its oscillations?

	Period/s	Frequency/Hz	
(A)	0.50	2.0	Ⓐ
(B)	2.0	0.25	Ⓑ
(C)	2.0	0.50	Ⓒ
(D)	20	0.025	Ⓓ

<u>Item 3</u> refers to the diagram below. The bob of the pendulum takes 0.15 seconds to swing from X to Y and then to O.

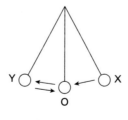

3 The frequency of its oscillation is

(A) 0.15 Hz   Ⓐ

(B) 5.0 s^{-1} Ⓑ

(C) 0.20 Hz   Ⓒ

(D) 0.80 s^{-1} Ⓓ

4 A simple pendulum consisting of a small bob suspended by a long, light string oscillates with small angular amplitude. Which of the following adjustments could result in it obtaining an increased period?

(A) Increasing the length of the string   Ⓐ

(B) Decreasing the length of the string   Ⓑ

(C) Decreasing the amplitude of the oscillations by a small amount   Ⓒ

(D) Using a bob of different mass   Ⓓ

Items **5–6** refer to the following graph.

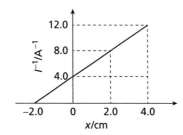

5 The value of I^{-1} when $x = 0$ is

(A) −2.0 cm   Ⓐ

(B) 4.0 A^{-1} Ⓑ

(C) 2.0 cm   Ⓒ

(D) 12.0 A^{-1} Ⓓ

6 The slope of the graph is

(A) 4.0 A^{-1} cm   Ⓐ

(B) 6.0 A^{-1} cm   Ⓑ

(C) 4.0 A^{-1} cm^{-1} Ⓒ

(D) 2.0 A^{-1} cm^{-1} Ⓓ

7 The width of a desk was measured using a metre rule having intervals of 1 mm. Which of the following is MOST appropriate for expressing the result?

(A) 0.524 m   (A)

(B) 0.5254 m   (B)

(C) 0.53 m   (C)

(D) 52 cm   (D)

8 A force of 290 N acts on an area of 1.2 m^2. A student uses his calculator, which displays the result as 241.6666667. The pressure is BEST represented as

(A) 241.6 Pa   (A)

(B) 240 Pa   (B)

(C) 242 Pa   (C)

(D) 241.666 6667 Pa   (D)

9 5.345 expressed to TWO significant figures is

(A) 5.35   (A)

(B) 5.4   (B)

(C) 5.3   (C)

(D) 53   (D)

10 The area of a rectangle of length 200 cm and width 80 cm is

(A) 1600 cm^2 (A)

(B) 16 000 m^2 (B)

(C) 1.6 m^2 (C)

(D) 160 cm^2 (D)

11 0.005 21 can be represented in scientific notation as

(A) 5.21×10^{3} Ⓐ

(B) 5.21×10^{-2} Ⓑ

(C) 5.21×10^{-3} Ⓒ

(D) 521×10^{-5} Ⓓ

12 The reason that some scales have a mirror behind the pointer is

(A) to reduce parallax error.   Ⓐ

(B) to reflect light and so enable it to be more easily seen.   Ⓑ

(C) to assist in estimating the distance between markings on the scale.   Ⓒ

(D) to magnify the space between the markings on the scale.   Ⓓ

13 Which of the following is/are true regarding linear and non-linear scales?

    I Linear scales are more accurate than non-linear scales.

    II Linear scales are straight whereas non-linear scales are curved.

    III It is more difficult to estimate readings on a non-linear scale because the distances between adjacent markings on a non-linear scale are different.

(A) I only   Ⓐ

(B) I and II only   Ⓑ

(C) II only   Ⓒ

(D) III only   Ⓓ

14 Which of the following measuring instruments is BEST for measuring the volume of a small, irregularly shaped stone?

(A) A burette   Ⓐ

(B) A measuring tape   Ⓑ

(C) A measuring cylinder   Ⓒ

(D) A micrometer screw gauge   Ⓓ

Item **15** refers to the following diagram of a Vernier caliper.

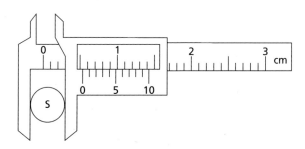

15 The diameter of the small sphere, S, is

(A) 0.8 cm   Ⓐ

(B) 0.53 mm   Ⓑ

(C) 0.53 cm   Ⓒ

(D) 1.4 cm   Ⓓ

Item **16** refers to the following diagram of a micrometer screw gauge.

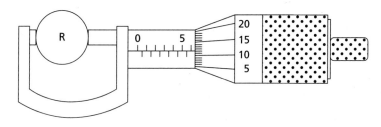

16 The diameter of the thin rod, R, being measured by the micrometer screw gauge is

(A) 5.62 mm   Ⓐ

(B) 5.5 mm   Ⓑ

(C) 6.0 mm   Ⓒ

(D) 6.12 mm   Ⓓ

17 The diameter of a cricket ball is BEST measured by

(A) a metre rule. Ⓐ

(B) a vernier caliper. Ⓑ

(C) a tape measure. Ⓒ

(D) a micrometer screw gauge. Ⓓ

18 Objects P and Q are placed in a bowl of water. P floats and Q sinks. Which one or more of the following can be deduced from this information?

    I Q is heavier than P.

    II 1 cm^3 of Q has a greater mass than 1 cm^3 of P.

    III Q is denser than water, and water is denser than P.

(A) I only Ⓐ

(B) I and II only Ⓑ

(C) II and III only Ⓒ

(D) I, II and III Ⓓ

Item **19** refers to the diagram below, which shows a measuring cylinder containing a liquid before and after a small object is immersed in it. The mass of the measuring cylinder and the liquid is 140 g. When the small object is added, the total mass becomes 200 g.

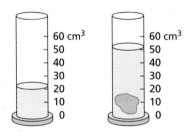

19 The density of the small object is

(A) 2.0 g cm^{-3} Ⓐ

(B) 0.5 g cm^{-3} Ⓑ

(C) 0.50 g cm^{-3} Ⓒ

(D) 60 g cm^{-3} Ⓓ

1 A dimensionless quantity has no unit. Which of the following quantities is NOT dimensionless?

(A) Magnification   Ⓐ

(B) Refractive index   Ⓑ

(C) Amplitude   Ⓒ

(D) Relative density   Ⓓ

2 Which of the following groups contains TWO fundamental quantities?

(A) Force, momentum, mass   Ⓐ

(B) Voltage, current, resistance   Ⓑ

(C) Pressure, quantity of substance, current   Ⓒ

(D) Velocity, refractive index, time   Ⓓ

3 Which of the following quantities is a derived quantity?

(A) Mass   Ⓐ

(B) Temperature   Ⓑ

(C) Energy   Ⓒ

(D) Current   Ⓓ

4 The SI base unit of temperature is

(A) the degree Fahrenheit.   Ⓐ

(B) the kelvin.   Ⓑ

(C) the degree centigrade.   Ⓒ

(D) the degree Celsius.   Ⓓ

5 The newton (N) is equivalent to

(A) $kg\ m^{-1}\ s^{2}$ Ⓐ

(B) $kg\ m\ s^{-2}$ Ⓑ

(C) $kg\ m^{-1}\ s^{-2}$ Ⓒ

(D) $kg\ m^{2}\ s^{2}$ Ⓓ

6 Which of the quantities is INCORRECTLY paired with its unit?

(A) Frequency / s^{-1} Ⓐ

(B) Resistance / $V\ A^{-1}$ Ⓑ

(C) Power / J s   Ⓒ

(D) Pressure / $N\ m^{-2}$ Ⓓ

7 Energy per second can be stated using

(A) the joule (J).   Ⓐ

(B) the volt (V).   Ⓑ

(C) the watt (W).   Ⓒ

(D) the hertz (Hz).   Ⓓ

8 25 kV can also be expressed as

(A) $25 \times 10^{6}\ mV$ Ⓐ

(B) $25 \times 10^{6}\ \mu V$ Ⓑ

(C) $25 \times 10^{-6}\ mV$ Ⓒ

(D) $25 \times 10^{-6}\ \mu V$ Ⓓ

9 Which of the following is a vector quantity?

(A) Mass   Ⓐ

(B) Pressure   Ⓑ

(C) Frequency   Ⓒ

(D) Displacement   Ⓓ

10 A scalar quantity is one that has

(A) magnitude and direction.   Ⓐ

(B) only magnitude.   Ⓑ

(C) mass but not weight.   Ⓒ

(D) only direction.   Ⓓ

<u>Item **11**</u> refers to the following diagram, which shows several forces acting on a small object.

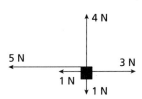 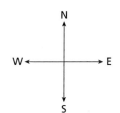

11 The direction of the object's acceleration is towards

(A) north-east.   Ⓐ

(B) south-east.   Ⓑ

(C) north-west.   Ⓒ

(D) south-west.   Ⓓ

Item **12** refers to the following diagram, which shows a force of 15 N acting at an angle of 30° above the horizontal.

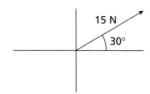

12 The vertical and horizontal components of this force are respectively

(A) 13 N and 7.5 N   Ⓐ

(B) 10 N and 5.0 N   Ⓑ

(C) 7.5 N and 13 N   Ⓒ

(D) 5.0 N and 10 N   Ⓓ

Item **13** refers to the following diagram, which shows forces of 12 N and 16 N acting on a particle, P, in directions due north and due west respectively.

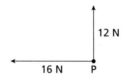

13 Which of the following BEST represents the resultant force?

Ⓐ

Ⓑ

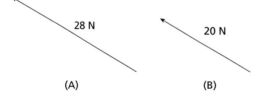

Ⓒ

Ⓓ

14 Which of the following diagrams BEST illustrates the summation of a 6 N force and an 8 N force acting at right angles to each other?

Ⓐ

Ⓑ

Ⓒ

Ⓓ

Item 15 refers to the following diagram, which shows two forces acting at a point P.

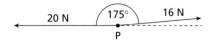

15 The resultant force is

(A) 4 N. Ⓐ

(B) 36 N. Ⓑ

(C) slightly less than 36 N. Ⓒ

(D) slightly more than 4 N. Ⓓ

16 Which of the following groups consists only of vectors?

(A) Displacement, velocity, pressure Ⓐ

(B) Momentum, force, velocity Ⓑ

(C) Displacement, force, speed Ⓒ

(D) Force, acceleration, work Ⓓ

A3 Statics

1 Two small copper spheres repel when placed close to each other on a horizontal surface. What type of force could be responsible for the repulsion?

(A) Magnetic force between two similar poles Ⓐ

(B) Electrostatic force between two similar charges Ⓑ

(C) Gravitational force between the masses Ⓒ

(D) Nuclear force between the nucleons in the copper Ⓓ

2 Which of the following is/are true?

    I The density of a stone depends on the acceleration due to gravity.

    II An object attached to a spring balance will produce a smaller reading on a planet where the acceleration due to gravity is less, but an object attached to a lever-arm balance will produce the same reading.

    III An object with a density of 0.9 relative to that of water will float.

(A) I and II only   Ⓐ

(B) I and III only   Ⓑ

(C) II and III only   Ⓒ

(D) III only   Ⓓ

3 Which of the following is true regarding the gravitational field strength near the surface of a given planet?

(A) It is the force of gravity acting on a body resting on the planet.   Ⓐ

(B) It is equivalent to the acceleration due to gravity on a body falling freely near to the surface of the planet in the absence of resistive forces.   Ⓑ

(C) It is greater on larger masses than it is on smaller masses resting on the planet.   Ⓒ

(D) It is measured in newtons.   Ⓓ

4 A rock is taken from the surface of Mars to the surface of Jupiter, where the gravitational field strength is much greater. Which of the following is true?

(A) The mass and the weight of the rock increase.   Ⓐ

(B) The mass of the rock increases but its weight remains the same.   Ⓑ

(C) The weight of the rock increases but its mass remains the same.   Ⓒ

(D) Neither the mass nor the weight of the rock changes, since the quantity of matter comprising the rock does not change.   Ⓓ

5 In which of the following devices is the effort (represented by an arrow) greater than the load being overcome?

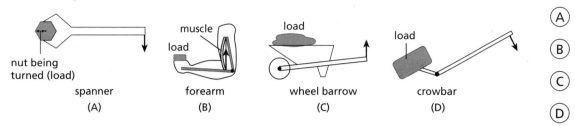

nut being
turned (load)

spanner
(A)

muscle
load

forearm
(B)

load

wheel barrow
(C)

load

crowbar
(D)

(A)
(B)
(C)
(D)

6 The centre of gravity of a body is

(A) the point at the geometric centre of the body.

(B) the point through which the total weight of the body acts.

(C) the point of application of the resultant force on the body due to gravity.

(D) the point on the body through which the total force of gravity acts.

(A)
(B)
(C)
(D)

7 Which of the following are true for a system of coplanar forces acting on a uniform metal rod in equilibrium?

    I The resultant force in any particular direction is zero.

    II The sum of the clockwise moments about the left end of the rod is equal to the sum of the anticlockwise moments about the left end of the rod.

    III The sum of the clockwise forces is equal to the sum of the anticlockwise forces about the pivot on which it rests.

    IV The sum of the clockwise moments about the centre of the rod is equal to the sum of the anticlockwise moments about the centre of the rod.

(A) I and III only

(B) II and III only

(C) I and IV only

(D) I, II and IV

(A)
(B)
(C)
(D)

Item **8** refers to the following diagram, which shows a uniform rod of length 1.0 m in equilibrium.

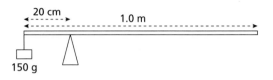

8 What is the weight of the rod?

(A) 0.10 N   Ⓐ

(B) 1.0 N   Ⓑ

(C) 10 N   Ⓒ

(D) 100 N   Ⓓ

Item **9** refers to the following diagram, which shows a uniform rod of weight W supported at one end by a fulcrum and suspended at the other end by a string. R and T are the reaction force from the fulcrum and the tension in the string respectively.

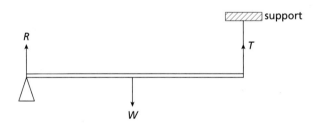

9 Which of the following are true?

    I $W - T = R$ **II** $T > W$ **III** $R = T$

(A) I and II only   Ⓐ

(B) II and III only   Ⓑ

(C) I and III only   Ⓒ

(D) I, II and III   Ⓓ

Item **10** refers to the following diagram, which shows a rod, pivoted on a fulcrum, in equilibrium under the action of forces *P*, *Q* and *R*. The letters *x*, *y* and *z* represent the distances shown on the diagram.

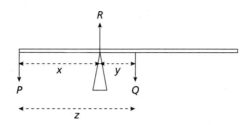

10 Which of the following is/are true?

$$\text{I } R - P = Q \qquad \text{II } Rx = Qy \qquad \text{III } Px = Qz$$

(A) I only ⒶA

(B) II only ⒷB

(C) I and II only ⒸC

(D) I and III only ⒹD

11 Which of the following is NOT true?

(A) When a body in stable equilibrium is slightly tilted, a moment is created but its weight continues to act through its base. ⒶA

(B) When a body in unstable equilibrium is slightly displaced, its centre of gravity falls. ⒷB

(C) Displacing a body in stable, unstable or neutral equilibrium always creates a moment. ⒸC

(D) On slightly displacing a body in neutral equilibrium, its centre of gravity remains at the same level. ⒹD

<u>Item 12</u> refers to the following graph, which shows how the load F applied to a spring varies with its extension e during an experiment.

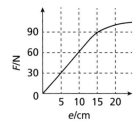

12 Which of the following is/are true?

    I The force constant of the spring during elastic deformation is 6.0 N cm^{-1}.

    II Hooke's law has been conformed to throughout the experiment.

    III A load of 60 N will produce an extension of 10 cm.

    IV The proportional limit was not exceeded.

(A) I only   Ⓐ

(B) II and III only   Ⓑ

(C) I and III only   Ⓒ

(D) III and IV only   Ⓓ

13 Which of the following will DEFINITELY increase the stability of an object?

    (A) Increasing the width of its base and raising its centre of gravity.   Ⓐ

    (B) Decreasing the width of its base and lowering its centre of gravity.   Ⓑ

    (C) Decreasing the width of its base and raising its centre of gravity.   Ⓒ

    (D) Increasing the width of its base and lowering its centre of gravity.   Ⓓ

Items **14–15** refer to a vertical spring. The lengths of the spring when loaded with forces of 20 N and 60 N are 15 cm and 25 cm respectively.

14 What is the force per unit extension of the spring?

(A) 1.3 N cm^{-1} Ⓐ

(B) 4.0 N cm^{-1} Ⓑ

(C) 2.4 N cm^{-1} Ⓒ

(D) 2.0 N cm^{-1} Ⓓ

15 What is the length of the spring if the load is completely removed?

(A) 5 cm   Ⓐ

(B) 10 cm   Ⓑ

(C) 15 cm   Ⓒ

(D) 20 cm   Ⓓ

A4 Kinematics

1 Akil was cycling at 4.0 m s^{-1} and then suddenly accelerated uniformly along a straight road. 5.0 s later he had acquired a velocity of 19.0 m s^{-1}. What was his acceleration?

(A) 0.33 m s^{-2} Ⓐ

(B) 75 m s^{-2} Ⓑ

(C) 3.0 m s^{-2} Ⓒ

(D) 3.8 m s^{-2} Ⓓ

2 A rubber ball travelling horizontally at 24 m s^{-1} strikes a vertical wall and rebounds with the same speed. What is the magnitude of its acceleration as it collides with the wall if the impact period is 0.12 s?

(A) 400 m s^{-2} (A)

(B) 0 m s^{-2} (B)

(C) 200 m s^{-2} (C)

(D) 4.0 m s^{-2} (D)

3 Kemal travels a distance of 36 km in a time of 2.0 hours. What is his speed in m s^{-1}?

(A) 5.0 m s^{-1} (A)

(B) 10 m s^{-1} (B)

(C) 18 m s^{-1} (C)

(D) 72 m s^{-1} (D)

<u>Items 4–5</u> refer to the following situation. A small object can travel along a straight track. It moves through a distance of 8.0 m in a time of 2.0 s, remains at rest for the next 12.0 s, and then returns along its path to its starting point in the next 6.0 s.

4 The average speed is

(A) 5.3 m s^{-1} (A)

(B) 2.7 m s^{-1} (B)

(C) 0.80 m s^{-1} (C)

(D) 0 m s^{-1} (D)

5 The average velocity is

(A) 5.3 m s^{-1} (A)

(B) 2.7 m s^{-1} (B)

(C) 0.80 m s^{-1} (C)

(D) 0 m s^{-1} (D)

Item **6** refers to the following displacement–time graph.

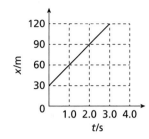

6 The velocity of the object is:

(A) 30 m s^{-1} (A)

(B) 40 m s^{-1} (B)

(C) 60 m s^{-1} (C)

(D) 45 m s^{-1} (D)

Item **7** refers to the following displacement–time graph.

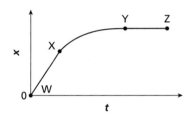

7 Which of the following BEST describes the velocity during the various stages?

	W to X	X to Y	Y to Z	
(A)	Increasing	Increasing	Constant	(A)
(B)	Increasing	Decreasing	Constant	(B)
(C)	Constant	Decreasing	Not zero	(C)
(D)	Constant	Decreasing	Zero	(D)

Item **8** refers to the following velocity–time graph.

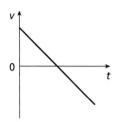

8 Which of the following could the motion represent?

(A) An object sliding down an incline.   Ⓐ

(B) An object falling from rest and then bouncing back up.   Ⓑ

(C) An object shot vertically into the air and then falling to its starting point.   Ⓒ

(D) An object moving in one direction only with a constant acceleration.   Ⓓ

Items **9–10** refer to the following velocity–time graph.

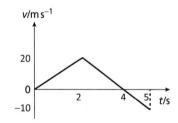

9 What is the distance travelled in the first 4 seconds?

(A) 10 m   Ⓐ

(B) 20 m   Ⓑ

(C) 30 m   Ⓒ

(D) 40 m   Ⓓ

10 What is the value of t when the object changes direction?

(A) 2 s   Ⓐ

(B) 4 s   Ⓑ

(C) 5 s   Ⓒ

(D) 7 s   Ⓓ

Items **11–12** refer to the following graph.

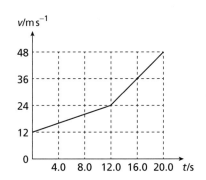

11 What is the acceleration during the last 8 seconds?

(A) 3.0 m s^{-2} (A)

(B) 2.4 m s^{-2} (B)

(C) 6.0 m s^{-2} (C)

(D) 192 m s^{-2} (D)

12 What is the distance travelled during the last 8 seconds?

(A) 96 m   (A)

(B) 192 m   (B)

(C) 290 m   (C)

(D) 504 m   (D)

13 An object is shot vertically into the air and then falls back along its path to the ground. Neglecting air resistance and buoyancy forces, which of the following BEST describes the object's acceleration?

(A) It decreases as the object rises and increases as the object falls.   (A)

(B) It is greater at the highest point than it is at the lowest point.   (B)

(C) It is momentarily zero at the highest point.   (C)

(D) It remains the same throughout the flight.   (D)

Items **14–15** refer to the following graphs, which show students' suggested representations of the motion of a heavy stone falling from the roof of a house.

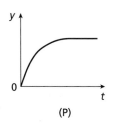
(P)

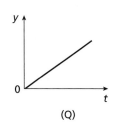
(Q)

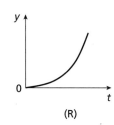
(R)

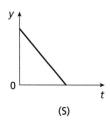
(S)

14 If *y* represents velocity, which graph BEST illustrates the motion?

(A) P   Ⓐ

(B) Q   Ⓑ

(C) R   Ⓒ

(D) S   Ⓓ

15 If *y* represents displacement, which graph BEST illustrates the motion?

(A) P   Ⓐ

(B) Q   Ⓑ

(C) R   Ⓒ

(D) S   Ⓓ

Item **16** refers to the following displacement–time graph.

16 Which of the following velocity–time graphs BEST illustrates the motion represented in the displacement–time graph?

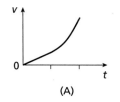
(A)

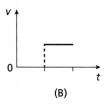
(B)

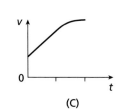
(C)

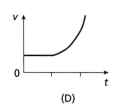
(D)

Ⓐ

Ⓑ

Ⓒ

Ⓓ

A5 Dynamics

1 The philosopher who believed that the force applied to a body is proportional to its velocity was

(A) Newton.   Ⓐ

(B) Galileo.   Ⓑ

(C) Aristotle.   Ⓒ

(D) Pascal.   Ⓓ

2 In which one or more of the following is the resultant force zero?

   I A heavy boat zooming across the water at constant velocity with its engine at full throttle.

   II A man with a parachute descending at constant velocity of 2 m s^{-1}.

   III A weather balloon hovering in one position over a mountain.

(A) I only   Ⓐ

(B) I and II only   Ⓑ

(C) II and III only   Ⓒ

(D) I, II and III   Ⓓ

3 An object of mass 500 g is pulled horizontally by a horizontal string. What is its acceleration if the tension in the string is 40 N and the frictional force acting is 8 N?

(A) 64 m s^{-2} Ⓐ

(B) 80 m s^{-2} Ⓑ

(C) 16 m s^{-2} Ⓒ

(D) 4 m s^{-2} Ⓓ

Item **4** refers to the following situations.

X: When a person jumps on a trampoline, the downward force they exert on it causes an upward force of equal magnitude from the trampoline onto the soles of their feet.

Y: During take-off, the back rest of the seat of an aircraft presses onto the passenger, causing him to accelerate.

Z: A spacecraft can travel through outer space at a high constant velocity even though the net force on it is zero.

4 Which of Newton's laws do these situations BEST demonstrate?

	X	Y	Z
(A)	1st law	2nd law	3rd law
(B)	2nd law	1st law	3rd law
(C)	3rd law	2nd law	1st law
(D)	1st law	3rd law	2nd law

Ⓐ Ⓑ Ⓒ Ⓓ

5 A ball of mass 400 g, moving horizontally to the left at 20 m s^{-1}, rebounds at 10 m s^{-1} from a vertical wall. What is the time of impact if the force of the wall on the ball is 600 N?

(A) 0.020 s   Ⓐ

(B) 0.050 s   Ⓑ

(C) 0.20 s   Ⓒ

(D) 0.50 s   Ⓓ

6 Two identical cars, A and B, are racing along a straight track. They both have constant velocity but A is travelling faster than B. Which of the following statements about the cars is/are true?

    I The total resistive force on A is greater than the total resistive force on B.

    II The resultant force on A is greater than the resultant force on B.

    III The resultant force on A and the resultant force on B are both zero.

(A) I only   Ⓐ

(B) II only   Ⓑ

(C) I and III only   Ⓒ

(D) III only   Ⓓ

7 Which of the following statements is/are true?

    I The total momentum of any closed system is constant.

    II The momentum of an object before a collision must be equal to its momentum after the collision.

    III It is possible for two colliding bodies to each have momentum before a collision and to each have zero momentum immediately after the collision.

(A) I only   Ⓐ

(B) I and II only   Ⓑ

(C) II and III only   Ⓒ

(D) I and III only   Ⓓ

8 A small object X moves at a velocity of 4 m s^{-1} and collides with another object Y of the same mass and initially at rest. X is brought instantly to rest. What is the velocity of Y after the collision?

(A) 0 m s^{-1} Ⓐ

(B) 2 m s^{-1} Ⓑ

(C) 4 m s^{-1} Ⓒ

(D) 8 m s^{-1} Ⓓ

9 A block of mass 2.0 kg moves horizontally to the right at 5.0 m s^{-1} and collides head on with a block of mass 3.0 kg which is moving to the left at 10 m s^{-1}. What is the total momentum before the collision?

(A) 20 kg m s^{-1} to the left   Ⓐ

(B) 40 kg m s^{-1} to the right   Ⓑ

(C) 40 kg m s^{-1} to the left   Ⓒ

(D) 20 kg m s^{-1} to the right   Ⓓ

<u>Item **10**</u> refers to the following diagram, which shows an object of mass m and speed v about to collide head-on with an object of mass $\dfrac{m}{2}$ and speed $2v$ travelling in the opposite direction.

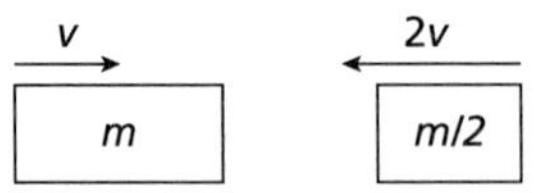

10 Assuming that the objects stick together, what is their common speed after the collision?

(A) $\dfrac{v}{2}$ Ⓐ

(B) $2v$ Ⓑ

(C) 0   Ⓒ

(D) $4v$ Ⓓ

A6 Energy

1 An electricity power station burns diesel so that it can boil water and produce steam to turn the turbine of a generator. Which of the following BEST gives the sequence of energy transfers that occur during the process?

(A) thermal ⇒ chemical ⇒ kinetic ⇒ electrical   Ⓐ

(B) chemical ⇒ thermal ⇒ kinetic ⇒ electrical   Ⓑ

(C) chemical ⇒ gravitational ⇒ kinetic ⇒ electrical   Ⓒ

(D) chemical ⇒ thermal ⇒ electric   Ⓓ

2 Which of the following BEST gives the sequence of energy transfers that occur at a hydroelectric power station?

(A) gravitational potential ⇒ electromagnetic ⇒ kinetic ⇒ electrical   Ⓐ

(B) chemical potential ⇒ kinetic ⇒ electrical   Ⓑ

(C) gravitational potential ⇒ heat and sound ⇒ electrical   Ⓒ

(D) gravitational potential ⇒ kinetic ⇒ electrical   Ⓓ

3 Which of the following groups contains an example of non-renewable energy?

(A) Wind energy/solar energy   Ⓐ

(B) Geothermal energy/energy from crude oil   Ⓑ

(C) Energy from biogas/tidal energy   Ⓒ

(D) Hydro energy of a waterfall/wave energy   Ⓓ

<u>Items 4–6</u> refer to the following situation. Kimran pushes horizontally on a block with a force of 800 N, moving it through a distance of 5.0 m across a level floor in a time of 20 s. Due to a frictional force, the block moves at constant velocity.

4 What work is done by Kimran in pushing the block?

(A) 40 J   Ⓐ

(B) 160 J   Ⓑ

(C) 4000 J   Ⓒ

(D) 16 000 J   Ⓓ

5 What part of this work is done against friction?

(A) 40 J   Ⓐ

(B) 160 J   Ⓑ

(C) 4000 J   Ⓒ

(D) 16 000 J   Ⓓ

6 What is the power used by Kimran?

(A) 200 W   Ⓐ

(B) 80 W   Ⓑ

(C) 800 W   Ⓒ

(D) 2.0 W   Ⓓ

7 Which of the following is NOT an example of potential energy?

(A) Energy released from a stretched elastic band.   Ⓐ

(B) Energy released on digesting a slice of bread.   Ⓑ

(C) Energy of a bullet due to its high speed.   Ⓒ

(D) Energy of a mango hanging from a tree.   Ⓓ

8 What is the maximum kinetic energy that can be acquired by a coconut of weight 32 N as it falls through a distance of 20 m?

(A) 1.6 J Ⓐ

(B) 1600 J Ⓑ

(C) 6400 J Ⓒ

(D) 640 J Ⓓ

9 Balls A and B of identical mass are rolling across a level surface at speeds v and $2v$ respectively. If the kinetic energy of A is 200 J, what is the kinetic energy of B?

(A) 800 J Ⓐ

(B) 400 J Ⓑ

(C) 200 J Ⓒ

(D) 100 J Ⓓ

10 A river meets the edge of a cliff and the water falls through a distance h. What is the value of h if the maximum speed of the water in its drop is 20 m s^{-1}?

(A) 10 m Ⓐ

(B) 20 m Ⓑ

(C) 30 m Ⓒ

(D) 40 m Ⓓ

11 A machine raises an object of weight 1200 N through a distance of 5.0 m. What is its efficiency if the energy input is 8000 J?

(A) 75% Ⓐ

(B) 80% Ⓑ

(C) 60% Ⓒ

(D) 25% Ⓓ

Items **12–13** refer to the following diagram, which shows a ball of mass 2.0 kg and speed v approaching an incline of height 4.0 m.

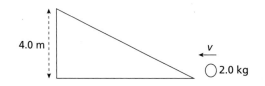

12 If the ball just makes it to the top of the incline, and no energy is lost to the surroundings, what is the value of v?

(A) 8.9 m s^{-1} Ⓐ

(B) 80 m s^{-1} Ⓑ

(C) 4.2 m s^{-1} Ⓒ

(D) 100 m s^{-1} Ⓓ

13 What is the gravitational potential energy of the ball at the top of the incline?

(A) 0.5 J   Ⓐ

(B) 80 J   Ⓑ

(C) 2 J   Ⓒ

(D) 8 J   Ⓓ

14 Which of the following is NOT a means to determine the efficiency of a machine?

(A) $\dfrac{\text{useful work output}}{\text{work input}}$ Ⓐ

(B) $\dfrac{\text{useful power output}}{\text{power input}}$ Ⓑ

(C) $\dfrac{\text{effort} \times \text{distance moved by effort}}{\text{load} \times \text{distance moved by load}}$ Ⓒ

(D) $\dfrac{\text{load} \times \text{distance moved by load}}{\text{effort} \times \text{distance moved by effort}}$ Ⓓ

Item **1** refers to the block shown in the following diagram. The weight of the block is 1200 N.

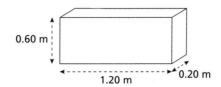

1 The block is turned so that it rests on a face which creates the maximum pressure. What is this pressure?

(A) 10 kPa   (A)

(B) 8.3 kPa   (B)

(C) 1.7 kPa   (C)

(D) 5 kPa   (D)

2 A fish is at a depth of 20 m in a lake on a day when the atmospheric pressure is 1.0×10^5 Pa. What is the total pressure on the fish if the density of the water in the lake is 1.0×10^3 kg m^{-3}?

(A) 2.0×10^5 Pa   (A)

(B) 3.0×10^5 Pa   (B)

(C) 1.5×10^5 Pa   (C)

(D) 3.0×10^4 Pa   (D)

3 Off-road vehicles that can travel on soft muddy terrain have very broad tyres. These tyres are used to ensure that

(A) the weight of the vehicle resting on the mud is reduced.   (A)

(B) the force exerted on the mud is reduced.   (B)

(C) the pressure that the vehicle creates on the mud is reduced.   (C)

(D) the upthrust on the tyres is increased.   (D)

4 On which TWO of the following does the pressure at the bottom of an aquarium depend?

    I The volume of water in the aquarium

    II The mass of the water in the aquarium

    III The density of the water

    IV The depth of the water

(A) I and II   Ⓐ

(B) II and III   Ⓑ

(C) II and IV   Ⓒ

(D) III and IV   Ⓓ

Item **5** refers to the following diagram. The block resting on piston Y is raised by applying a downward force at piston X.

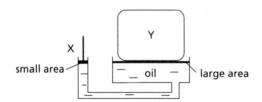

5 Which of the following is/are true when a downward force is applied at X to raise the block at Y?

    I The force exerted at X must be equal to or greater than the weight of the block.

    II The downward force exerted at X is smaller than the upward force it creates at Y.

    III The increase in pressure at X is equal to the increase in pressure created at Y.

(A) I only   Ⓐ

(B) II only   Ⓑ

(C) II and III only   Ⓒ

(D) III only   Ⓓ

Item **6** refers to the following diagram, which shows a simple mercury barometer.

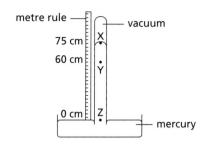

6 What are the pressures (in cm Hg) at X, Y and Z?

	X	Y	Z
	Pressure/cm Hg		
(A)	75	90	150
(B)	75	60	0
(C)	0	15	75
(D)	15	60	75

Ⓐ Ⓑ Ⓒ Ⓓ

Item **7** refers to the following diagram, which shows a simple manometer containing a liquid of density 5000 kg m^{-3}.

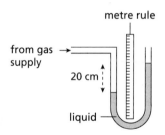

7 What is the pressure of the gas supply if the atmospheric pressure is 1.0×10^5 Pa?

(A) 1.1×10^5 Pa Ⓐ

(B) 1.0×10^4 Pa Ⓑ

(C) 1.0×10^6 Pa Ⓒ

(D) 1.1×10^6 Pa Ⓓ

8 A small mass is attached to a spring balance by means of a string and is lowered into a beaker of water until it is completely submerged. The reading on the balance is reduced

(A) until it is equal to the weight of water displaced.   Ⓐ

(B) by an amount equal to the weight of water displaced.   Ⓑ

(C) by an amount equal to the weight of the object.   Ⓒ

(D) to zero since the mass is now stationary.   Ⓓ

9 Which of the following is/are true for an object floating in a fluid?

    I The upthrust is equal to the weight of fluid displaced.

    II The weight of the object is equal to the weight of the fluid displaced.

    III The resultant force on the object is zero.

(A) I only   Ⓐ

(B) II only   Ⓑ

(C) I and II only   Ⓒ

(D) I, II and III   Ⓓ

10 A weather balloon accelerates upward into the air. Which of the following statements is/are true?

    I The weight of the balloon is less than the weight of the air displaced.

    II The weight of the air displaced is equal to the weight of the balloon.

    III The weight of the balloon is less than the upthrust on it.

(A) I only   (A)

(B) II only   (B)

(C) I and III only   (C)

(D) II and III only   (D)

11 An object of mass 200 g and volume 250 cm^3 floats in a liquid of density 1.6 g cm^{-3}. What is the volume of the part of the object that is submerged?

(A) 125 cm^3 (A)

(B) 320 cm^3 (B)

(C) 400 cm^3 (C)

(D) 25 cm^3 (D)

Section B: Thermal Physics and Kinetic Theory
B1 Nature of heat, macroscopic properties and phenomena

1 Which of the following are true concerning early theory on the nature of heat?

    I Heat was believed to be an invisible fluid called 'caloric', which could combine with matter and raise its temperature.

    II When bodies were heated and changed state, a change in caloric could not be detected.

    III Count Rumford's 'cannon boring' experiment provided evidence for the caloric theory.

    IV In the 18th century, the caloric theory replaced the kinetic theory of matter.

(A) I and II only   Ⓐ

(B) II and III only   Ⓑ

(C) I, II and III only   Ⓒ

(D) III and IV only   Ⓓ

2 Which scientist demonstrated the relationship between work done and energy transferred and thereby established the principle of conservation of energy?

(A) Rumford   Ⓐ

(B) Joule   Ⓑ

(C) Watt   Ⓒ

(D) Newton   Ⓓ

3 Which of the following is NOT true of a liquid-in-glass clinical thermometer?

(A) The liquid it contains cannot be alcohol.   Ⓐ

(B) Its range is from 20 °C to 50 °C.   Ⓑ

(C) Its bore has a narrow constriction so that the liquid remains in the stem when the thermometer is removed from the patient.   Ⓒ

(D) It is shaken between uses so that liquid in the stem can be returned to the bulb for the next use.   Ⓓ

4 Which of the following is/are true with respect to heat and temperature?

    I Heat can flow from body P to body Q even if P contains less thermal energy than Q.

    II If body P is at a higher temperature than body Q, then P contains more thermal energy than Q.

    III Heat is thermal energy in the process of transfer from places of higher temperature to places of lower temperature due to a temperature difference between them.

(A) I and II only   Ⓐ

(B) I and III only   Ⓑ

(C) II and III only   Ⓒ

(D) III only   Ⓓ

5 Which of the following is NOT true?

(A) On the Celsius scale, the upper fixed point is the temperature of steam from pure boiling water at standard atmospheric pressure.   Ⓐ

(B) Temperature is a form of energy that flows between points having different amounts of heat.   Ⓑ

(C) The boiling point of water at the top of a mountain is lower than it is at the bottom.   Ⓒ

(D) On the Celsius scale, the lower fixed point is the temperature of pure melting ice at standard atmospheric pressure.   Ⓓ

6 Which of the following BEST describes the range of a clinical thermometer?

(A) 0 °C ➡ 100 °C   Ⓐ

(B) –10 °C ➡ 110 °C   Ⓑ

(C) 20 °C ➡ 40 °C   Ⓒ

(D) 35 °C ➡ 43 °C   Ⓓ

7 Which of the following are true with respect to the design of a liquid-in-glass thermometer?

    I A thin-walled bulb will produce a faster response time than a thick-walled bulb.

    II If it contains alcohol, it will respond faster than if it contains mercury.

    III If it has a larger bulb and a correspondingly longer stem, the thermometer would be more sensitive.

    IV The thinner the bore, the greater is the precision or sensitivity of the thermometer.

(A) I and III   (A)

(B) II and III   (B)

(C) I, III and IV   (C)

(D) II, III and IV   (D)

8 Which of the following is/are true with respect to thermometers?

    I A thermoelectric thermometer has a larger range of measurement than a liquid-in-glass mercury thermometer.

    II A mercury thermometer responds faster than a thermoelectric thermometer.

    III The thermometric property utilised by a thermoelectric thermometer is the emf it produces when there is a temperature difference between its junctions.

(A) I only   (A)

(B) I and II   (B)

(C) I and III only   (C)

(D) II and III   (D)

9 Which of the following is NOT true of the kinetic theory of matter?

(A) Strong intermolecular forces exist between molecules that are very close to each other. Ⓐ

(B) The molecules of an ideal gas have only kinetic energy; they have no potential energy. Ⓑ

(C) The temperature of an ideal gas depends on the kinetic energy of its molecules. Ⓒ

(D) All molecules of a particular gas have the same speed. Ⓓ

10 Which of the following is/are true with respect to the phases of matter?

I The molecules of a liquid are packed close together and therefore liquids are difficult to compress.

II The molecules of solids and liquids have potential and kinetic energy but the molecules of an ideal gas only have kinetic energy.

III Liquids flow because the intermolecular forces between their particles are very strong, and when any particle moves forward it pulls others along with it.

(A) I and II only Ⓐ

(B) II only Ⓑ

(C) II and III only Ⓒ

(D) I and III only Ⓓ

11 Which of the following is/are true of Brownian motion?

I It is the random motion of the molecules of a liquid or gas.

II It increases with increased temperature.

III It is caused by the bombardment of small, light particles, suspended in a liquid or gas, by molecules of the liquid or gas.

(A) I only Ⓐ

(B) I and II only Ⓑ

(C) II and III only Ⓒ

(D) I, II and III Ⓓ

Item 12 refers to the following diagram, which shows a bimetallic strip comprised of brass and invar. The left end of the strip is fixed and is attached to an insulating support.

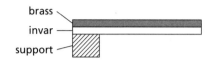

brass
invar
support

12 Brass expands more than invar when heated. Which of the following is/are true?

    I Raising the temperature causes the right end of the strip to move downward.

    II When heated, the brass gets hotter than the invar, and therefore expands more.

    III Brass must be a better conductor than invar.

    (A) I only   (A)

    (B) I and II only   (B)

    (C) II and III only   (C)

    (D) I, II and III   (D)

13 Which of the following is NOT true?

    (A) 300 K = 27 °C   (A)

    (B) 0 K = 273 °C   (B)

    (C) –73 °C = 200 K   (C)

    (D) 10 °C = 283 K   (D)

14 Which of the following graphs correctly relates the pressure p with the thermodynamic temperature T of a fixed mass of an ideal gas at constant volume?

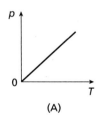 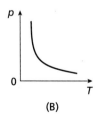 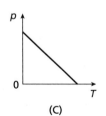 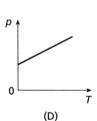

    (A)   (B)   (C)   (D)

(A)

(B)

(C)

(D)

15 Which of the following graphs correctly relates the variation of volume V with Celsius temperature θ of a fixed mass of an ideal gas at constant pressure?

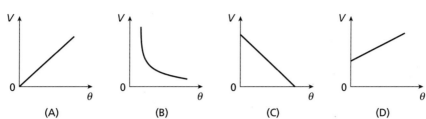

(A)   (B)   (C)   (D)

Ⓐ Ⓑ Ⓒ Ⓓ

16 Which of the following graphs correctly relates the variation of pressure p and volume V of a fixed mass of an ideal gas at constant temperature?

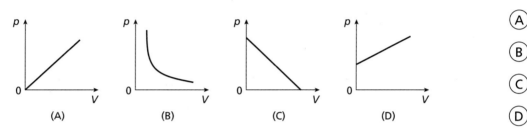

(A)   (B)   (C)   (D)

Ⓐ Ⓑ Ⓒ Ⓓ

17 A bubble rises from the bottom of a lake 30 m deep and is four times its original volume just before breaking the surface. If the temperature is constant and the pressure at the bottom of the lake is p, what is the pressure at the water surface?

(A) $4p$

(B) $30p$

(C) $\dfrac{1}{4}p$

(D) $\dfrac{1}{30}p$

Ⓐ Ⓑ Ⓒ Ⓓ

18 A gas at a temperature of 127 °C is heated in a freely expandable container until its volume doubles. What is the new temperature of the gas?

(A) 254 °C

(B) 527 °C

(C) 254 K

(D) 527 K

Ⓐ Ⓑ Ⓒ Ⓓ

19 Which of the following is/are true of Charles' law?

    I A change of volume of the gas occurs at constant pressure.

    II The volume of the gas is directly proportional to its Celsius temperature.

    III The ratio of the volume of the gas to its thermodynamic temperature is constant at constant pressure.

(A) I only   Ⓐ

(B) I and III only   Ⓑ

(C) II and III only   Ⓒ

(D) I, II and III   Ⓓ

20 The pressure of a gas in a strong steel container increases when heated because

(A) a larger number of molecules strike the walls of the container.   Ⓐ

(B) the volume of the gas increases.   Ⓑ

(C) the molecules of the gas make stronger and more frequent collisions with the walls of the container because they travel at higher speeds.   Ⓒ

(D) Each molecule expands and therefore larger molecules are creating greater pressure.   Ⓓ

21 A gas is *slowly* pumped into a strong, rigid, good conducting vessel. Which of the following is true?

(A) The temperature of the gas will rise.   Ⓐ

(B) The rate of collisions between the molecules of the gas and the container will increase.   Ⓑ

(C) The pressure increases since the speed of the molecules increases.   Ⓒ

(D) The volume of gas will increase.   Ⓓ

22 Which one or more of the following properties of a gas MUST be constant when verifying the pressure law?

     I Pressure   **II** Temperature   **III** Volume   **IV** Mass

(A) I only   Ⓐ

(B) I and II   Ⓑ

(C) I and IV only   Ⓒ

(D) III and IV only   Ⓓ

Item **23** refers to the following diagram, which shows the typical apparatus used to verify one of the ideal gas laws.

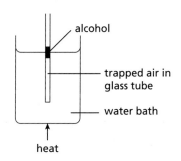

23 On applying heat, the bead of alcohol moves and then becomes steady once more. Which of the following is true with respect to the change in state of the trapped air?

(A) Its pressure remains the same as initially, but its volume has increased.   Ⓐ

(B) Its pressure and volume have both increased.   Ⓑ

(C) Its volume has increased and therefore its pressure has decreased.   Ⓒ

(D) Its volume has increased and therefore the mass of air has increased.   Ⓓ

1 The heat released per unit temperature when a block of copper cools is its

(A) specific heat of cooling. (A)

(B) specific heat capacity. (B)

(C) heat capacity. (C)

(D) latent heat. (D)

2 Which of the following is true of the heat capacity of a body?

(A) It is the heat required to raise the temperature of 1 kg of the substance by 1 K. (A)

(B) It is the heat released when the temperature of 1 kg of the substance falls by 1 K. (B)

(C) It depends on the mass of the body. (C)

(D) Its SI unit of measurement is $J\,kg^{-1}\,K^{-1}$. (D)

3 A, B, C and D are beakers of liquids whose masses and specific heat capacities are represented in terms of m and c respectively. Which of the liquids would experience the GREATEST temperature rise if they are each given the same amount of heat?

(A)

(B)

m, c $m, 2c$ $2m, c$ $2m, 2c$

(A)   (B)   (C)   (D)

(C)

(D)

4 Which of the following is the unit of specific heat capacity?

(A) $J\,kg^{-1}$ (A)

(B) $kg\,K^{-1}$ (B)

(C) $J\,kg^{-1}\,K^{-1}$ (C)

(D) $kg\,J^{-1}$ (D)

5 A heater of power 500 W is used to warm a mass of 2.0 kg of liquid by 20 °C in a time of 4.0 minutes. Using this data, the specific heat capacity of the liquid is

(A) $50 \, J \, kg^{-1} \, K^{-1}$ (A)

(B) $3000 \, J \, kg^{-1} \, K^{-1}$ (B)

(C) $12\,000 \, J \, kg^{-1} \, K^{-1}$ (C)

(D) $500 \, J \, kg^{-1} \, K^{-1}$ (D)

6 Which of the following is the unit of latent heat?

(A) J (A)

(B) $J \, kg^{-1} \, K^{-1}$ (B)

(C) $J \, K^{-1}$ (C)

(D) $kg \, J^{-1}$ (D)

7 The unit for the specific latent heat of vaporisation is

(A) $J \, kg^{-1}$ (A)

(B) $kg \, K^{-1}$ (B)

(C) $J \, kg^{-1} \, K^{-1}$ (C)

(D) $J \, K^{-1}$ (D)

8 Which of the following is/are true concerning the change of phase of a substance?

I The specific latent heat of fusion of a substance is the heat needed to change the substance from solid to liquid without a change of temperature.

II The latent heat of vaporisation of a body is the heat needed to change unit mass of the body from liquid to gas without a change of temperature.

III When latent heat is released from a body, its molecules lose potential energy.

(A) I only   (A)

(B) II only   (B)

(C) III only   (C)

(D) I, II and III   (D)

Items **9–11** refer to the following graph, which shows the change of phase of a substance.

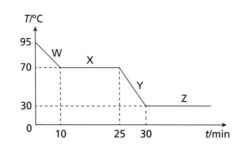

9 In which section of the graph is the substance in the gaseous phase?

(A) W Ⓐ

(B) X Ⓑ

(C) Y Ⓒ

(D) Z Ⓓ

10 What is the boiling point of the substance?

(A) 30 °C Ⓐ

(B) 70 °C Ⓑ

(C) 95 °C Ⓒ

(D) 368 K Ⓓ

11 Which of the following is NOT true as the experiment proceeds?

(A) The kinetic energy of the particles of the substance decreases during stage W. Ⓐ

(B) The kinetic energy of the particles of the substance decreases during stage X. Ⓑ

(C) The potential energy of the particles of the substance decreases during stage Z. Ⓒ

(D) After solidifying, the substance was not further cooled. Ⓓ

Item **12** refers to the following diagram, which shows ice being melted by an electric heater and the mass of the molten ice being measured.

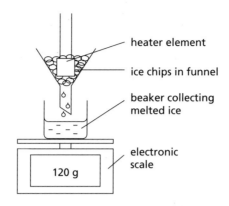

12 If the power of the heater is P and a mass m of water was formed in the beaker in a time t, what is the specific latent heat of fusion of the ice?

(A) $\dfrac{Pm}{t}$ Ⓐ

(B) $\dfrac{Pt}{m}$ Ⓑ

(C) $\dfrac{m}{Pt}$ Ⓒ

(D) $\dfrac{Pm}{t}$ Ⓓ

13 1.0 kg of water of specific heat capacity 4200 J kg^{-1} K^{-1} is heated from 10 °C until it completely boils and changes to gas. If the specific latent heat of vaporisation of water is 2.3×10^6 J kg^{-1}, what is the thermal energy provided?

(A) 3.8×10^6 J   Ⓐ

(B) 3.8×10^5 J   Ⓑ

(C) 2.7×10^6 J   Ⓒ

(D) 2.7×10^5 J   Ⓓ

14 For which change will the rate of evaporation from a wet towel NOT increase?

(A) Increased surface area   Ⓐ

(B) Increased humidity   Ⓑ

(C) Increased temperature   Ⓒ

(D) Increased wind   Ⓓ

15 Which of the following is/are true concerning evaporation and boiling?

   I Boiling occurs throughout a liquid whereas evaporation only occurs at its surface.

   II Evaporation occurs over a range of temperatures whereas boiling only occurs at one temperature for a given pressure.

   III An external heat source must constantly provide energy to a liquid during the processes of evaporation and boiling.

(A) I only   Ⓐ

(B) II only   Ⓑ

(C) I and II only   Ⓒ

(D) I, II and III   Ⓓ

16 Which of the following concerning evaporation and/or condensation is/are true?

   I Earthenware pots keep their contents cool because liquid in the tiny pores of the vessel constantly evaporates, drawing latent heat of vaporisation from its contents.

   II When perspiration evaporates from our skin, it absorbs latent heat of vaporisation from our bodies.

   III The refrigerant in a freezing compartment of a fridge condenses and thereby cools the food within it as it absorbs latent heat of vaporisation.

(A) I only   Ⓐ

(B) I and II only   Ⓑ

(C) II only   Ⓒ

(D) II and III only   Ⓓ

1 In which of the following is heat transferred MAINLY by conduction?

(A) Being warmed by standing a few metres away from a bonfire.   Ⓐ

(B) Being warmed when looking face down from a roof into an active chimney.   Ⓑ

(C) Ironing a shirt with an electric iron.   Ⓒ

(D) Cooking a piece of tuna on a barbeque grill.   Ⓓ

<u>Item 2</u> refers to the following diagram, which shows a piece of ice trapped in the bottom of a test tube of water that is being heated at the top.

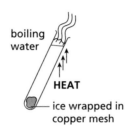

2 It is observed that the water boils at the top of the tube long before the ice begins to melt. Which one or more of the following is/are the reason(s) for this?

   I Water is a poor conductor of heat.

   II The copper is a good conductor and conducts heat away from the ice.

   III Natural convection currents cannot bring hot water downward.

(A) I only   Ⓐ

(B) I and II only   Ⓑ

(C) I and III only   Ⓒ

(D) II and III   Ⓓ

3 The following diagrams each show a beaker of water being heated at one side of its base. Which of the diagrams BEST illustrates the direction of the convection currents produced?

Ⓐ
Ⓑ
Ⓒ
Ⓓ

heat   heat   heat   heat

(A)   (B)   (C)   (D)

4 Which of the following is/are true about conduction in metals and non-metals?

    I Metals are better conductors than non-metals because they contain more electrons.

    II In metals and non-metals, thermal energy is conducted by vibrating particles bombarding each other and transferring their kinetic energy.

    III Free translating electrons exist in metals, and on bombardment with metallic cations, kinetic energy can be transferred to or from these electrons.

(A) I and II only   Ⓐ

(B) I and III only   Ⓑ

(C) II and III only   Ⓒ

(D) III only   Ⓓ

5 Which of the following is/are true of the various types of energy transfer?

    I Convection is the process of heat transfer between two points in a medium by the movement of the particles of the medium due to existing regions of different density.

    II Conduction is the process of heat transfer between two points in a medium by the relaying of energy between adjacent particles of the medium.

    III Thermal radiation is electromagnetic radiation; hot bodies emit radiation of longer wavelengths than do cooler bodies.

(A) I only   Ⓐ

(B) I and II only   Ⓑ

(C) II and III only   Ⓒ

(D) I, II and III   Ⓓ

6 By which of the following processes does a thermos flask, built with a vacuum in its walls, reduce thermal energy transfer?

(A) Conduction and radiation only Ⓐ

(B) Radiation only Ⓑ

(C) Conduction and convection only Ⓒ

(D) Conduction, convection and radiation Ⓓ

7 Water at 0 °C is added to two black cans and two silver cans up to the levels shown in the following diagrams. In which can will the water warm to the surrounding room temperature of 30 °C soonest?

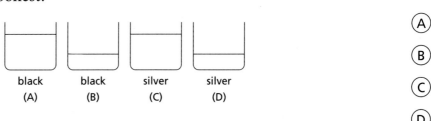

| black | black | silver | silver |
| (A) | (B) | (C) | (D) |

Ⓐ
Ⓑ
Ⓒ
Ⓓ

8 Which of the following statements involving thermal radiation is/are true?

   I When working in a large freezer room, wearing a white coat will keep you warmer than wearing a black coat.

  II A white fridge will keep its contents cooler than a black fridge.

 III An oven with white outer walls will keep its contents warmer than one with black outer walls.

(A) I and II only Ⓐ

(B) II only Ⓑ

(C) II and III only Ⓒ

(D) I, II and III Ⓓ

9 Which of the following is NOT true concerning thermal radiation?

(A) A cool black surface is a better absorber of radiation than a white or silver surface at the same temperature. (A)

(B) A hot silver surface is a better emitter of thermal radiation than a black surface at the same temperature. (B)

(C) Thermal radiation can propagate through a vacuum. (C)

(D) A rough, dull black surface emits radiation better than a smooth, shiny black surface at the same temperature. (D)

10 Global warming is due to the greenhouse effect, where the atmosphere behaves like the glass of the greenhouse. Which of the following gases are NOT greenhouse gases?

(A) Carbon dioxide (A)

(B) Methane and chlorofluorocarbons (B)

(C) Oxygen (C)

(D) Water vapour (D)

11 Which of the following is/are true with respect to a greenhouse (sometimes called a glasshouse)?

    I High frequency waves and some of the more energetic infrared waves emitted from the very hot Sun can penetrate the glass of the greenhouse and warm the plants inside.

    II Lower frequency infrared waves emitted by the lower temperature objects inside the greenhouse are unable to penetrate the glass and leave.

    III By keeping the walls and roof sealed, convection of the hot air to the surroundings prevents the greenhouse from becoming too hot.

(A) I only (A)

(B) II only (B)

(C) I and II only (C)

(D) I, II and III (D)

12 Which of the following does NOT cause hot air to rise?

(A) An increase in the volume of the air   Ⓐ

(B) An increase in the density of the air   Ⓑ

(C) A displacement of the hot air by cooler air   Ⓒ

(D) An increase in the speed of the air molecules   Ⓓ

13 Which of the following is NOT true concerning a solar water heater?

(A) Its tubes are made of copper because copper is a good thermal conductor and can transfer the energy quickly to the water they contain.   Ⓐ

(B) The heater panel is covered by glass to trap infrared radiation that would otherwise leave.   Ⓑ

(C) The heater panel is placed above the storage tank to allow the flow of water by a natural convection current.   Ⓒ

(D) The panel is placed on a slope so that the heated water can rise within it and be delivered from its higher end to the storage tank.   Ⓓ

Section C: Waves and Optics
C1 Wave motion

1 The speed of the motor of a vibrator of a ripple tank is increased.
The waves produced will have

(A) increased speed. (A)

(B) decreased speed. (B)

(C) increased wavelength. (C)

(D) decreased wavelength. (D)

2 Which of the following statements about waves is NOT true?

(A) Vibrations in a transverse wave are perpendicular to the progression of the wave. (A)

(B) Progressive waves transfer energy from one point to the next. (B)

(C) All waves travel at 3.0×10^8 m s^{-1} in a vacuum. (C)

(D) Transverse and longitudinal waves can exhibit the phenomena of reflection, refraction, diffraction and interference. (D)

3 Which of the following types of waves is longitudinal?

(A) Microwaves (A)

(B) Sound waves (B)

(C) Light waves (C)

(D) Water waves (D)

4 Which of the following is NOT true of a longitudinal progressive wave?

(A) It has compressions and rarefactions, which are places of high and low pressure respectively. (A)

(B) The distance from a compression to the nearest rarefaction is one wavelength. (B)

(C) It can only travel through a material medium. (C)

(D) Each particle in the wave vibrates to and fro along the line of propagation. (D)

Items **5–7** refer to the following graph, which shows the relation between displacement *x* and time *t* for the oscillations of a wave.

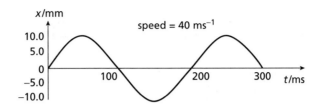

5 The frequency of the wave is

(A) 100 Hz   Ⓐ

(B) 200 Hz   Ⓑ

(C) 5.0 Hz   Ⓒ

(D) 10.0 Hz   Ⓓ

6 The wavelength of the wave is

(A) 8.0 m   Ⓐ

(B) 200 m   Ⓑ

(C) 0.20 m   Ⓒ

(D) 100 m   Ⓓ

7 The amplitude of the wave is

(A) 20 mm   Ⓐ

(B) 10 mm   Ⓑ

(C) 200 mm   Ⓒ

(D) 100 mm   Ⓓ

Item **8** refers to the following graph of displacement against position for a wave.

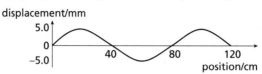

8 The speed of the wave is 32 m s^{-1}. What is its frequency?

(A) 80 Hz   (A)

(B) 0.80 Hz   (B)

(C) 40 Hz   (C)

(D) 0.40 Hz   (D)

Item **9** refers to the following diagram, which shows layers of air vibrating due to a longitudinal wave.

9 Which of the following distances is the wavelength of the wave?

(A) A to B   (A)

(B) C to E   (B)

(C) A to D   (C)

(D) E to G   (D)

Item **10** refers to the following diagram.

10 Which of the following pairs of particles are NOT in phase?

(A) R and U   (A)

(B) S and V   (B)

(C) T and U   (C)

(D) Q and W   (D)

Item **11** refers to the following diagram, which shows a water wave drawn full scale. The broken line represents the mean position of the vibrating particles.

11 Which of the following diagrams, also drawn full scale, shows a wave that has greater amplitude but lower frequency than the wave above?

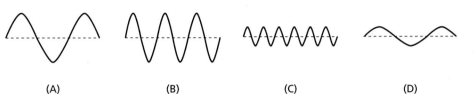

(A)   (B)   (C)   (D)

Ⓐ
Ⓑ
Ⓒ
Ⓓ

C2 Sound waves and electromagnetic waves

1 Which of the following is NOT true of sound waves?

(**A**) They are formed by a vibrating body.   Ⓐ

(**B**) They must be propagated through a material medium.   Ⓑ

(**C**) The direction of propagation is parallel to the direction in which the particles of the medium oscillate.   Ⓒ

(**D**) Sounds in the audible range having a high pitch travel faster through air than those with a low pitch.   Ⓓ

2 The frequency of a note increases with its

(**A**) wavelength.   Ⓐ

(**B**) loudness.   Ⓑ

(**C**) pitch.   Ⓒ

(**D**) velocity.   Ⓓ

3 The amplitude of a sound wave governs its

(A) loudness. (A)

(B) wavelength. (B)

(C) pitch. (C)

(D) speed. (D)

4 Which of the following ranges of frequencies is correctly classified?

	Audible sound	Ultrasound	Infrasound
(A)	20 Hz ⟹ 20 kHz	>20 kHz	<20 Hz
(B)	20 Hz ⟹ 20 kHz	<20 Hz	>20 kHz
(C)	<20 Hz	>20 kHz	20 Hz ⟹ 20 kHz
(D)	>20 kHz	20 Hz ⟹20 kHz	<20 Hz

(A)
(B)
(C)
(D)

5 A transmitter on a ship sends out an ultrasound signal to the sea bed in order to determine the depth of water at its location. After a period of 1.2 s the receiver detects the returning echo. If the speed of sound in the water is 1500 m s^{-1}, what is the depth of the water?

(A) 1800 m (A)

(B) 204 m (B)

(C) 2500 m (C)

(D) 900 m (D)

6 A blast of thunder is heard 6.0 s after the flash of lightning from the same cloud is seen. How far away is the storm cloud if the speed of sound in air is 333 m s^{-1}?

(A) 2.0 km (A)

(B) 56 km (B)

(C) 18 km (C)

(D) 0.018 km (D)

Item 7 refers to the following graph, which shows how the vibrations of a sound wave vary with time.

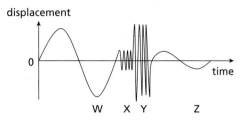

7 Which of the following BEST describes note X?

	Volume	**Pitch**
(A)	high	low
(B)	low	high
(C)	high	high
(D)	low	low

Ⓐ Ⓑ Ⓒ Ⓓ

8 Jennifer shouts at the top of her voice and seconds later hears a faint echo. The loudness has diminished because the returning wave now

(A) travels slower.

(B) has a decreased amplitude.

(C) has a decreased frequency.

(D) has a smaller distance between its compressions.

Ⓐ Ⓑ Ⓒ Ⓓ

9 Which of the following is NOT true of sound waves?

(A) They are longitudinal waves.

(B) Sound waves in the audible range of humans have frequencies much greater than light waves.

(C) Conversations are heard better at night because sound waves moving away from the ground continuously refract in a curved path until they return to the cooler air below.

(D) Sound travels faster in solids than it does in air.

Ⓐ Ⓑ Ⓒ Ⓓ

10 The nimble fingers of Mr DeFreitas produce a rapid flow of changing notes from his guitar. Which property of the sound waves produced does NOT change?

(A) Speed   Ⓐ

(B) Period   Ⓑ

(C) Loudness   Ⓒ

(D) Wavelength   Ⓓ

11 Which of the following is NOT true of electromagnetic waves?

(A) All electromagnetic waves travel at the same speed of 3.0×10^8 m s^{-1} in a vacuum.   Ⓐ

(B) Electromagnetic waves, unlike sound waves, do not require a material medium for their propagation.   Ⓑ

(C) Thermal radiation is not a form of electromagnetic radiation.   Ⓒ

(D) Red light has a larger wavelength than blue light in any given medium.   Ⓓ

12 Which of the following shows electromagnetic waves listed in order of decreasing wavelength?

(A) X-rays, ultraviolet, visible light, radio   Ⓐ

(B) Infrared, visible light, gamma, ultraviolet   Ⓑ

(C) Radio, visible light, ultraviolet, X-ray   Ⓒ

(D) Ultraviolet, gamma, X-ray, infrared   Ⓓ

13 Which of the following is NOT true of the wavelengths of electromagnetic waves?

(A) Electromagnetic waves of wavelength greater than 1 mm are radio waves.   Ⓐ

(B) Infrared waves have a smaller wavelength than visible light waves.   Ⓑ

(C) Visible light waves vary in wavelength from red (about 700 nm) to violet (about 400 nm).   Ⓒ

(D) X-rays have wavelengths that are less than 10 nm.   Ⓓ

14 When electromagnetic waves pass through a vacuum they MUST all have the same

(A) frequency.   (A)

(B) speed.   (B)

(C) wavelength.   (C)

(D) amplitude.   (D)

15 A radio wave has a wavelength of 400 m and a frequency of 7.5×10^5 Hz in air. What is the frequency of another radio wave that has wavelength 500 m in the same medium?

(A) 6.0×10^5 Hz   (A)

(B) 8.0×10^4 Hz   (B)

(C) 9.4×10^5 Hz   (C)

(D) 1.3×10^5 Hz   (D)

16 Which of the following are true of the uses of electromagnetic waves?

    I Ultraviolet radiation is used to treat certain skin disorders and also to make fluorescent materials glow.

    II Gamma waves can be used in treating cancer and in sterilising equipment.

    III Infrared waves are used for heating and also in photography to detect differences in surface temperatures.

    IV X-rays are used for producing images of our bones and also in crystallography.

(A) I and II only   (A)

(B) II and III only   (B)

(C) II, III, and IV only   (C)

(D) I, II, III and IV   (D)

17 Which of the following is NOT true of the sources that can produce electromagnetic radiation?

(A) Ultraviolet radiation is produced by the Sun, electric sparks, lightning and very hot objects such as arc-welding torches.   (A)

(B) X-rays are produced by unstable radioactive materials.   (B)

(C) Radio waves are produced at aerials in transmitter circuits.   (C)

(D) Infrared radiation is produced by all bodies; the higher the temperature, the greater is the amount of infrared radiation emitted.   (D)

C3 Light waves: wave–particle duality, shadows and reflection

1 In the beginning of the 18th century there were two rival theories of light: wave theory and particle (or corpuscular) theory. All but one of the scientists listed below supported the wave theory. Which scientist supported the particle theory?

(A) Newton   (A)

(B) Huygens   (B)

(C) Young   (C)

(D) Foucault   (D)

2 When a wave passes through a gap that is approximately as wide as the wave's wavelength, it spreads in the region it enters. What is this phenomenon called?

(A) Interference   (A)

(B) Refraction   (B)

(C) Diffraction   (C)

(D) Reflection   (D)

3 Which of the following is NOT true of diffraction?

(A) The diffraction of light waves is not observed often, because the wavelength of light is much smaller than most gaps normally encountered.   (A)

(B) Radio waves undergo significant diffraction due to their large wavelength.   (B)

(C) Blue light diffracts more than red light on passing through a given gap.   (C)

(D) All waves can undergo diffraction.   (D)

4 When constructive interference occurs due to two waves, it MUST be that

(A) the crests of the two waves are meeting.   (A)

(B) the vibrations of the two waves meet in phase.   (B)

(C) a crest of one wave is meeting a trough of the other.   (C)

(D) a compression of one wave is meeting a compression of the other.   (D)

<u>Item 5</u> refers to the following diagram. X and Y show the positions of two people who communicate by means of radio waves of wavelength about 1 km.

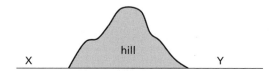

5 What wave phenomenon makes this communication possible even though the hill is intercepting the shortest direct path the waves can take?

(A) Reflection   (A)

(B) Refraction   (B)

(C) Dispersion   (C)

(D) Diffraction   (D)

6 Which of the following is NOT true of Young's double-slit experiment?

(A) The slits must be very narrow since the wavelength of light is very small.   (A)

(B) The experiment provides evidence for the particle theory of light.   (B)

(C) The slits must act as coherent sources for the interference pattern to be produced.   (C)

(D) The source should be of one colour to obtain a regular pattern of fringes on the screen.   (D)

7 In a Young's double-slit experiment, complete destructive interference occurs at a point where the vibrations from two wave sources meet with a path difference of

(A) $\frac{1}{4}$ wavelength.   (A)

(B) $\frac{1}{2}$ wavelength.   (B)

(C) $\frac{3}{4}$ wavelength.   (C)

(D) 0 wavelength.   (D)

8 Which of the following is true of Young's double-slit experiment?

(A) A bright fringe is produced when the optical path difference between the waves from the two sources is equal to $\frac{1}{2}\lambda$, $1\frac{1}{2}\lambda$, $2\frac{1}{2}\lambda$, etc.   (A)

(B) The fringe separation increases if the distance between the slits decreases.   (B)

(C) The central fringe is a dark fringe.   (C)

(D) When the optical path difference is a whole number of wavelengths, a dark fringe is produced.   (D)

9 Which of the following pairs of phenomena contribute to the interference pattern produced on the screen when performing a Young's double-slit experiment?

(A) Dispersion and reflection   (A)

(B) Refraction and diffraction   (B)

(C) Diffraction and interference   (C)

(D) Interference and refraction   (D)

<u>Items **10–11**</u> refer to the following diagram, which shows circular wavefronts from sources S_1 and S_2 crossing one another. The circles represent crests of the waves.

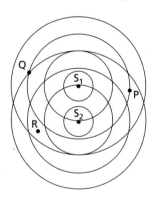

10 What type of interference occurs at each of the points P, Q and R?

	P	Q	R	
(A)	destructive	constructive	constructive	Ⓐ
(B)	destructive	destructive	constructive	Ⓑ
(C)	constructive	constructive	destructive	Ⓒ
(D)	constructive	destructive	destructive	Ⓓ

11 When the sources are operated individually, the amplitude of each of the waves is 2 mm. What are the displacements at P, Q and R at the instant shown in the diagram? (Upward from the mean position is taken as positive displacement.)

	P	Q	R	
(A)	2 mm	4 mm	4 mm	Ⓐ
(B)	0 mm	4 mm	0 mm	Ⓑ
(C)	0 mm	4 mm	−4 mm	Ⓒ
(D)	2 mm	0 mm	−4 mm	Ⓓ

12 Which of the following does NOT provide evidence to support the rectilinear propagation of light?

(A) An eclipse of the Sun   Ⓐ

(B) The shadow cast by a football on the field 4 metres below it   Ⓑ

(C) The fine beam of a laser through the air   Ⓒ

(D) A rainbow   Ⓓ

13 Amoka and her friend view the image of a book in a plane vertical mirror, from two different points in a room. Which one or more of the following does the position of the image they see depend on?

    I The distance of the person perpendicularly from the mirror.

    II The angle of the person's line of sight to the mirror.

    III The distance of the book from the mirror.

(A) I only   Ⓐ

(B) I and II only   Ⓑ

(C) II and III only   Ⓒ

(D) III only   Ⓓ

14 Which of the following is NOT a characteristic of an image formed in a plane mirror?

(A) It is the same size as the object.   Ⓐ

(B) It is the same distance perpendicularly behind the mirror as the object is in front.   Ⓑ

(C) It is real.   Ⓒ

(D) It is laterally inverted.   Ⓓ

Item **15** refers to the following diagram which shows light reflecting from two mirrors. The diagram is not drawn to scale.

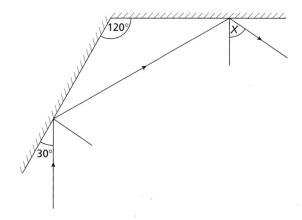

15 The angle of reflection X from the second mirror is

(A) 70°   Ⓐ

(B) 60°   Ⓑ

(C) 30°   Ⓒ

(D) 40°   Ⓓ

16 Algi stands facing a mirror with his arms stretched horizontally in front of him. His fingertips are 2.0 m from the mirror and the image of his fingertips appears to be 4.6 m from him. How far from the mirror is he standing?

(A) 4.0 m   Ⓐ

(B) 2.6 m   Ⓑ

(C) 6.6 m   Ⓒ

(D) 2.3 m   Ⓓ

17 Which of the following is NOT true of shadows?

(A) The shadow produced by a point source is a total shadow with a sharp, well defined edge.   Ⓐ

(B) The shadow produced by an extended source has an umbra and a penumbra.   Ⓑ

(C) Shadows are a direct result of the rectilinear propagation of light.   Ⓒ

(D) The intensity of light in a penumbra is the same at all points within it.   Ⓓ

18 Which of the following statements in relation to eclipses is NOT true?

(A) During an eclipse of the Sun, the Moon blocks the light from the Sun, preventing it from reaching Earth. Ⓐ

(B) During an eclipse of the Moon, the Moon blocks light from reaching Earth. Ⓑ

(C) An eclipse of the Moon occurs when it enters the umbra of the Earth. Ⓒ

(D) When a total solar eclipse is observed from a particular region on Earth, there are other regions from which only a partial solar eclipse is experienced. Ⓓ

19 Which of the following is/are true of the pinhole camera?

  I It is evidence of the straight-line (rectilinear) propagation of light.

  II It cannot take focused photos of moving objects.

  III Compared to a lens camera, a relatively long time must elapse before sufficient light energy can enter the camera to produce a suitable image on the film.

  IV A larger hole allows more light into the camera and therefore produces a brighter, more focused image.

(A) I only Ⓐ

(B) I and II only Ⓑ

(C) I, II and III only Ⓒ

(D) II, III and IV only Ⓓ

C4 Light waves: refraction, critical angle and total internal reflection

1 Which of the following is NOT true of refraction?

(A) The angle of incidence is equal to the angle of refraction. Ⓐ

(B) The incident ray, the refracted ray and the normal at the point of incidence are on the same plane. Ⓑ

(C) Snell's law states that the ratio $\dfrac{\text{sine (angle of incidence)}}{\text{sine (angle of refraction)}}$ is constant for a given pair of media. Ⓒ

(D) The ratio $\dfrac{\text{sine (angle of incidence)}}{\text{sine (angle of refraction)}}$ is known as the refractive index of the second medium relative to the first. Ⓓ

2 Which of the following is NOT true of a virtual image?

(A) It cannot be formed on a screen. Ⓐ

(B) The beam entering the eye from a virtual image is divergent. Ⓑ

(C) A virtual image can only be formed in a mirror. Ⓒ

(D) Light energy is not focused where the image appears to be. Ⓓ

3 Which of the following is unchanged by the refraction of a ray approaching a second medium at an angle other than 90° to its surface?

(A) Speed Ⓐ

(B) Wavelength Ⓑ

(C) Frequency Ⓒ

(D) Direction Ⓓ

4 The separation of white light into its constituent colours is known as

(A) reflection. Ⓐ

(B) diffraction. Ⓑ

(C) dispersion. Ⓒ

(D) interference. Ⓓ

5 Which of the following is/are true in relation to the refraction of light through the opposite sides of a rectangular glass block?

    I There is no net deviation of the ray.

    II There is no lateral displacement of the ray.

    III The ray undergoes two deviations, one clockwise and the other counterclockwise as it passes through the block.

(A) I only   Ⓐ

(B) II and III only   Ⓑ

(C) III only   Ⓒ

(D) I and III only   Ⓓ

6 Anil looked into the water from his canoe and found that the reef appeared closer to the surface than it actually was. This occurrence is due to

(A) reflection.   Ⓐ

(B) refraction.   Ⓑ

(C) diffraction.   Ⓒ

(D) interference.   Ⓓ

7 Which scientist first showed that white light was a mixture of radiations of different colours?

(A) Huygens   Ⓐ

(B) Snell   Ⓑ

(C) Newton   Ⓒ

(D) Young   Ⓓ

Item **8** refers to the following situation. White light is separated into its constituent colours on passing through a glass prism, as shown in the diagram.

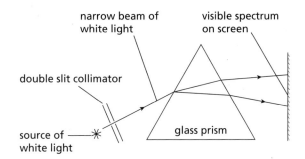

8 Which of the following is/are true?

  I The colour that deviates least on passing through the prism is violet.

  II The colour that refracts most is violet.

  III If a broad beam were used instead of a narrow one, the colours would recombine and the spectrum would not be seen.

  IV The speed and wavelength of light in glass are lowest for the colour that deviates most.

(**A**) I only   Ⓐ

(**B**) I and III only   Ⓑ

(**C**) II and III only   Ⓒ

(**D**) II, III and IV only   Ⓓ

9 A water wave has a speed of 2.4 m s^{-1}, which changes to 2.0 m s^{-1} as it passes over a sand bank where the depth of the water decreases. What is the refractive index of the region of shallower depth relative to the deeper region?

(**A**) 1.2   Ⓐ

(**B**) 0.8   Ⓑ

(**C**) 3.2   Ⓒ

(**D**) 8.0   Ⓓ

Items **10–12** refer to the following diagram, which shows a ray of light passing from material X to air.

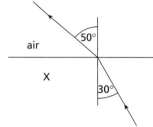

10 What is the refractive index of X?

(**A**) 1.2

(**B**) 1.5

(**C**) 0.78

(**D**) 1.4

Ⓐ

Ⓑ

Ⓒ

Ⓓ

11 If the speed of light in air is 3.0×10^8 m s^{-1}, what is its speed in X?

(**A**) 3.9×10^8 m s^{-1}

(**B**) 4.6×10^8 m s^{-1}

(**C**) 2.3×10^8 m s^{-1}

(**D**) 2.0×10^8 m s^{-1}

Ⓐ

Ⓑ

Ⓒ

Ⓓ

12 If the wavelength of the light in air is 6.0×10^{-7} m, what is its wavelength in X?

(**A**) 3.3×10^{-7} m

(**B**) 7.7×10^{-7} m

(**C**) 4.0×10^{-7} m

(**D**) 3.9×10^{-7} m

Ⓐ

Ⓑ

Ⓒ

Ⓓ

13 Which of the following is NOT true concerning waves refracting into a second medium?

(A) The speed of light in glass is lower than it is in water. Ⓐ

(B) The speed of sound in glass is lower than it is in water. Ⓑ

(C) The frequency and period of a wave are unchanged when the wave refracts. Ⓒ

(D) The wavelength of light in glass is smaller than it is in water. Ⓓ

14 Which of the following diagrams BEST shows the path of the ray of light through the glass prism?

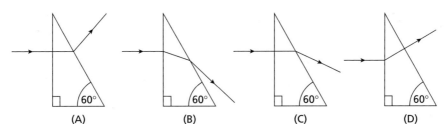

(A)   (B)   (C)   (D)

Ⓐ
Ⓑ
Ⓒ
Ⓓ

15 Which diagram BEST illustrates the dispersion of a narrow beam of white light by a glass prism?

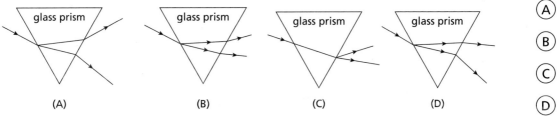

(A)   (B)   (C)   (D)

Ⓐ
Ⓑ
Ⓒ
Ⓓ

16 The refractive index η of a material of critical angle c with respect to air can be calculated from

(A) $\eta = \sin c$ Ⓐ

(B) $\eta = \dfrac{1}{\sin c}$ Ⓑ

(C) $\eta = \dfrac{90}{\sin c}$ Ⓒ

(D) $\eta = \dfrac{c}{90}$ Ⓓ

17 The refractive index of a material with respect to air is 1.3. Its critical angle with respect to air is

(A) 75°   Ⓐ

(B) 0.77°   Ⓑ

(C) 50°   Ⓒ

(D) 25°   Ⓓ

18 Which of the following diagrams correctly shows a ray of light approaching an interface between X and air, if the critical angle of material X is c?

Ⓐ

Ⓑ

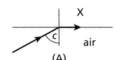 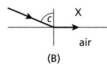 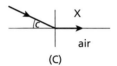 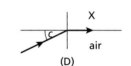

Ⓒ

Ⓓ

19 Which of the following is NOT true in relation to critical angle and total internal reflection?

(A) Total internal reflection can only occur in the medium of greater refractive index.   Ⓐ

(B) Total internal reflection can only occur if the angle of approach to the interface between the media is less than the critical angle.   Ⓑ

(C) Total internal reflection can only occur in the medium in which the wave travels more slowly.   Ⓒ

(D) For an air–water interface, total internal reflection of sound will occur in the air.   Ⓓ

Item **20** refers to the following diagram, which shows a small, glowing light bulb on the sea bed. Light can only exit the surface from within the disc of radius r as shown.

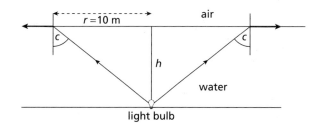

20 If the critical angle of the water is 49°, the depth h of the water is

(A) 8.7 m   Ⓐ

(B) 13 m   Ⓑ

(C) 12 m   Ⓒ

(D) 15 m   Ⓓ

21 Which of the following is NOT true with respect to the use of total internal reflection?

(A) Total internal reflection is utilised in cables made of glass fibres to transmit digital signals in our communication systems, such as telephone networks and the internet.   Ⓐ

(B) Fibre-optic cables can be used by doctors to transmit light into difficult areas such as the stomach or colon so that they can carry out surgery.   Ⓑ

(C) Periscopes use two right-angled isosceles glass prisms to reflect light by total internal reflection from above the water into submarines.   Ⓒ

(D) Repeated total internal reflection occurs in a fibre-optic cable where light travels at 3.0×10^8 m s^{-1}.   Ⓓ

1 Which of the following is/are true of the principal focus of a lens?

    I It is a point on the principal axis.

    II All light passing through a convex lens will converge through its principal focus.

    III A beam of rays, parallel to the principal axis, will appear to diverge from the principal focus after passing through a concave lens.

(A) I only   Ⓐ

(B) I and II only   Ⓑ

(C) I and III only   Ⓒ

(D) II and III only   Ⓓ

2 Which of the following is/are true of the focal plane of a lens?

    I It is perpendicular to the principal axis.

    II It contains the principal focus.

    III All parallel rays meeting a convex lens will pass through the same point on the focal plane after passing through the lens.

(A) I only   Ⓐ

(B) I and II only   Ⓑ

(C) II and III only   Ⓒ

(D) I, II and III   Ⓓ

3 The image formed by a concave lens is

(A) larger than the object.   Ⓐ

(B) further from the lens than is the object.   Ⓑ

(C) never inverted.   Ⓒ

(D) real.   Ⓓ

Items **4–8** refer to the following diagram of a convex lens of principal focus F.

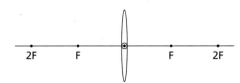

4 At what distance from the lens centre must an object be placed to produce a real, inverted, magnified image?

(A) Closer than F   Ⓐ

(B) Between F and 2F   Ⓑ

(C) At 2F   Ⓒ

(D) Further than 2F   Ⓓ

5 At what distance from the lens centre must an object be placed to produce a real, inverted, diminished image?

(A) Closer than F   Ⓐ

(B) Between F and 2F   Ⓑ

(C) At 2F   Ⓒ

(D) Further than 2F   Ⓓ

6 At what distance from the lens centre must an object be placed to produce a real, inverted, image that is the same size and distance from the lens as is the object?

(A) Closer than F   Ⓐ

(B) Between F and 2F   Ⓑ

(C) At 2F   Ⓒ

(D) Further than 2F   Ⓓ

7 At what distance from the lens centre is the object placed when the lens is being used in each of the following instruments?

	Camera	Projector	Magnifying glass
(A)	Between F and 2F	Further than 2F	Closer than F
(B)	Further than 2F	Between F and 2F	Closer than F
(C)	Further than 2F	Closer than F	At F
(D)	Closer than F	At 2F	Between F and 2F

Ⓐ Ⓑ Ⓒ Ⓓ

8 For the image formed by a convex lens to be real, the object must be placed

(A) closer to the lens than F. Ⓐ

(B) between F and 2F. Ⓑ

(C) further from the lens than F. Ⓒ

(D) further from the lens than 2F. Ⓓ

9 At which point in the following diagram will the parallel beam converge?

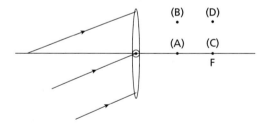

Ⓐ Ⓑ Ⓒ Ⓓ

Items **10–12** refer to the following situation. An object of height 2.0 cm is placed on the principal axis, 50.0 cm from a convex lens of focal length 20.0 cm.

10 What is the distance of the image from the lens?

(A) 33 cm Ⓐ

(B) 45 cm Ⓑ

(C) 60 cm Ⓒ

(D) 18 cm Ⓓ

11 What is the magnification of the image?

(A) 0.67   Ⓐ

(B) 0.40   Ⓑ

(C) 2.5   Ⓒ

(D) 0.80   Ⓓ

12 What is the height of the image?

(A) 5.0 cm   Ⓐ

(B) 2.5 cm   Ⓑ

(C) 1.3 cm   Ⓒ

(D) 1.0 cm   Ⓓ

13 A concave lens of focal length 12.0 cm is used to form an image of an object placed 8.0 cm from it. What is the distance of the image from the lens?

(A) 8.4 cm   Ⓐ

(B) 12 cm   Ⓑ

(C) 24 cm   Ⓒ

(D) 4.8 cm   Ⓓ

14 Which of the following incident rays directed towards a converging lens will refract to the point P as shown? (The point F is the principal focus.)

Ⓐ

Ⓑ

Ⓒ

Ⓓ

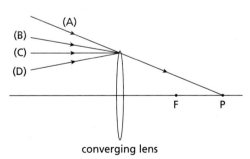

converging lens

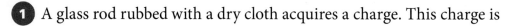

Section D: Electricity and Magnetism
D1 Electrostatics

1 A glass rod rubbed with a dry cloth acquires a charge. This charge is

(A) positive, and is due to protons transferring from the cloth to the rod. Ⓐ

(B) negative, and is due to electrons transferring from the cloth to the rod. Ⓑ

(C) positive, and is due to electrons transferring from the rod to the cloth. Ⓒ

(D) negative, and is due to protons transferring from the rod to the cloth. Ⓓ

2 A polythene rod rubbed with a dry cloth acquires a charge. This charge is

(A) positive, and is due to protons transferring from the cloth to the rod. Ⓐ

(B) negative, and is due to electrons transferring from the cloth to the rod. Ⓑ

(C) positive, and is due to electrons transferring from the rod to the cloth. Ⓒ

(D) negative, and is due to protons transferring from the rod to the cloth. Ⓓ

3 The following diagram shows three charges, X, Y and Z, each of the same magnitude and in positions that form an equilateral triangle. Charges X and Y are fixed in position, but Z can easily move. The arrows represent possible initial directions of the motion of Z. In which direction will Z start to move?

Ⓐ

Ⓑ

Ⓒ

Ⓓ

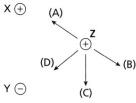

4 In which of the following diagrams can the arrangement produce a uniform electric field?

Ⓐ

Ⓑ

Ⓒ

Ⓓ

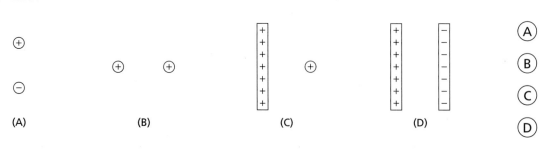

5 When a positively charged rod is brought near to a small uncharged piece of aluminium foil, the foil is attracted towards the rod. Which one or more of the following take place during the process?

    I Protons are repelled to the side of the foil furthest from the rod.

    II Electrons are attracted to the side of the foil closest to the rod.

    III A negative and a positive pole are induced in the foil, but its net charge is still zero (until it touches the rod).

    (A) I and II only   Ⓐ

    (B) II only   Ⓑ

    (C) II and III only   Ⓒ

    (D) I, II and III   Ⓓ

<u>Items **6–7**</u> refer to the following diagram, which shows the electric field around two charged spheres.

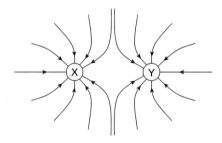

6 Which of the following is true?

    (A) Both charges are positive.   Ⓐ

    (B) X is positive and Y is negative.   Ⓑ

    (C) Both charges are negative.   Ⓒ

    (D) X is negative and Y is positive.   Ⓓ

7 Which of the following correctly indicates the direction of the force on each of the spheres?

	On X	On Y	
(A)	To the right	To the left	Ⓐ
(B)	To the left	To the left	Ⓑ
(C)	To the left	To the right	Ⓒ
(D)	To the right	To the right	Ⓓ

8 What charge develops on the following materials when rubbed with a dry cloth?

	Polythene	Perspex	Glass	
(A)	+	–	+	Ⓐ
(B)	+	+	–	Ⓑ
(C)	–	–	+	Ⓒ
(D)	–	+	+	Ⓓ

<u>Item **9**</u> refers to the following diagram, which shows an oil drop, P, suspended by an electric field between charged parallel metal plates, X and Y. The drop is at rest, so the weight of the drop must be equal to the upward force on it caused by the field.

P suspended
between charged
metal plates, X and Y

—————————————— X

● P

—————————————— Y

9 If the charges on X and Y are of the same magnitude, what are the possible signs of the charges on X, Y and P?

	X	Y	P	
(A)	+	–	+	Ⓐ
(B)	+	+	–	Ⓑ
(C)	–	+	+	Ⓒ
(D)	–	+	–	Ⓓ

1 In which of the following are the materials correctly categorised?

	Insulators	Semiconductors	Conductors	
(A)	Graphite (carbon)	Silicon	Mercury	Ⓐ
(B)	Glass	Plastic, silicon	Gold, copper	Ⓑ
(C)	Silicon	Copper	Aluminium	Ⓒ
(D)	Rubber, wood	Germanium	Silver, graphite	Ⓓ

2 Which of the following is NOT true of conductors, semiconductors and insulators?

(A) Conductors are materials that have more electrons than insulators. Ⓐ

(B) Insulators are materials in which electric charges cannot flow freely. Ⓑ

(C) Negative and positive charge carriers are responsible for the currents in semiconductors and in electrolytes such as sulfuric acid in a car battery. Ⓒ

(D) Electrons are the free charges in conductors that are responsible for the current. Ⓓ

3 Which of the following is/are true about charge and current?

I The direction of electron flow is opposite to that of conventional current and is therefore opposite to the direction in which a positive charge will move if free to do so.

II The SI unit of current is the coulomb.

III Electric charge is the rate of flow of current.

(A) I only Ⓐ

(B) II and III only Ⓑ

(C) III only Ⓒ

(D) I and III only Ⓓ

4 A charge of 15 µC flows for a period of 3.0 s. The current is:

(A) 5.0 µA   Ⓐ

(B) 0.20 A   Ⓑ

(C) 45 µA   Ⓒ

(D) 0.20 µA   Ⓓ

5 Which of the following statements about alternating current is NOT true?

(A) It is unsuitable for charging a battery.   Ⓐ

(B) Direct current flows in one direction only, but alternating current repeatedly reverses direction.   Ⓑ

(C) A semiconductor diode can be used to rectify alternating current to direct current.   Ⓒ

(D) It is not the form of electricity that is distributed by the electrical power company.   Ⓓ

<u>Item 6</u> refers to the following graph, which shows the variation of an alternating current I with time t.

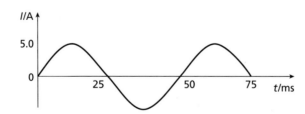

6 What are the period and frequency, respectively, of the alternating current?

(A) 75 ms, 0.013 Hz   Ⓐ

(B) 50 ms, 20 Hz   Ⓑ

(C) 25 ms, 40 Hz   Ⓒ

(D) 50 s, 5.0 Hz   Ⓓ

7 Which of the following graphs shows an alternating voltage?

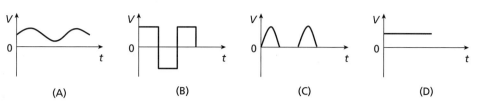

(A)   (B)   (C)   (D)

(A)
(B)
(C)
(D)

8 Which of the following equations of electrical quantities is correct?

(A) $Q = \dfrac{E}{V}$

(B) $P = \dfrac{V}{R^2}$

(C) $I = \dfrac{V}{P}$

(D) $Q = \dfrac{I}{t}$

(A)
(B)
(C)
(D)

9 What is the electrical energy required to move a charge of 40 µC through a resistor that has a potential difference of 12 V across it?

(A) 3.3 µJ

(B) 3×10^5 J

(C) 4.8×10^{-4} J

(D) 2.4×10^{-4} J

(A)
(B)
(C)
(D)

Items **10–12** refer to the following situation. A power of 500 W is used by a resistor for a period of 4.0 s when a current of 2.0 A flows through it.

10 What is the potential difference across the resistor?

(A) 1000 V

(B) 2000 V

(C) 125 V

(D) 250 V

(A)
(B)
(C)
(D)

11 What is the resistance of the resistor?

(A) 250 Ω   Ⓐ

(B) 1000 Ω   Ⓑ

(C) 125 Ω   Ⓒ

(D) 2000 Ω   Ⓓ

12 What is the energy consumed in the 4.0 s?

(A) 1000 J   Ⓐ

(B) 500 J   Ⓑ

(C) 250 J   Ⓒ

(D) 2000 J   Ⓓ

13 A resistance R uses a power P when a potential difference V is placed across it. What is the new power consumed if the voltage is doubled and the resistance is unchanged?

(A) $V^2 R$ Ⓐ

(B) $2P$ Ⓑ

(C) $\dfrac{V^2}{R}$ Ⓒ

(D) $4P$ Ⓓ

1 Which of the following is/are true of the zinc–carbon cell?

    I The current it delivers is due to reaction between the zinc case and the electrolyte of ammonium chloride gel.

    II Manganese(IV) oxide is placed around the carbon rod to prevent oxygen from collecting around it and increasing the internal resistance.

    III The positive pole is the graphite rod, and the negative pole is the zinc case.

(A) I only   Ⓐ

(B) II and III only   Ⓑ

(C) III only   Ⓒ

(D) I and III only   Ⓓ

<u>Item 2</u> refers to the following diagram, which shows a circuit being used to charge a 12 V accumulator from the ac 110 V mains supply.

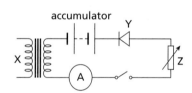

2 Which of the following is true of the circuit?

(A) X is a step-down transformer.   Ⓐ

(B) Y is a semiconductor diode connected so that current flowing through the accumulator is in the same direction as it would flow when it is discharging.   Ⓑ

(C) Y rectifies the dc to ac.   Ⓒ

(D) Z is a fuse that protects the circuit from excessive current.   Ⓓ

3 Which of the following is NOT true of the zinc–carbon dry cell and the lead–acid accumulator?

(A) The terminal voltages obtainable from a lead–acid cell and a zinc–carbon cell are, respectively, about 2 V and 1.5 V.   Ⓐ

(B) The lead–acid cell can produce a much larger current than the zinc–carbon cell.   Ⓑ

(C) The internal resistance of the lead–acid cell is about 0.5 Ω; that of the zinc–carbon cell is only about 0.01 Ω.   Ⓒ

(D) The lead–acid cell is rechargeable, but the zinc–carbon cell is not.   Ⓓ

4 The capacity of a 12 V battery is stated as 80 Ah. The energy it can store is

(A) 24 kJ   Ⓐ

(B) 960 J   Ⓑ

(C) 288 kJ   Ⓒ

(D) 3.5 MJ   Ⓓ

<u>Item 5</u> refers to the following graphs, which show the *I–V* characteristics of three components.

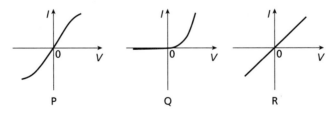

5 The components are:

	P	**Q**	**R**	
(A)	Metallic resistor	Filament lamp	Semiconductor diode	Ⓐ
(B)	Semiconductor diode	Filament lamp	Metallic resistor	Ⓑ
(C)	Filament lamp	Semiconductor diode	Metallic resistor	Ⓒ
(D)	Metallic resistor	Semiconductor diode	Filament lamp	Ⓓ

Item **6** refers to the following *I–V* graph of a resistor.

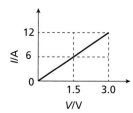

6 What is its resistance?

   (A) 4.0 Ω   Ⓐ

   (B) 0.25 Ω   Ⓑ

   (C) 36 Ω   Ⓒ

   (D) 2.0 Ω   Ⓓ

7 Which of the following is NOT true of resistance?

   (A) It is the ratio of the pd across a conductor to the current through it.   Ⓐ

   (B) It is the opposition provided to an electric current.   Ⓑ

   (C) If a material obeys Ohm's law, its resistance is directly proportional to the pd across it.   Ⓒ

   (D) The resistance of a filament lamp increases as the current increases.   Ⓓ

Item **8** refers to the following diagram showing the connections between resistors W, X, Y and Z.

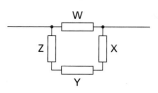

8 Which of the following is NOT true of the resistors W, X, Y and Z?

   (A) The total resistance is less than the sum of X, Y and Z.   Ⓐ

   (B) The total resistance is less than the resistance of W.   Ⓑ

   (C) W is in parallel with the group, X, Y and Z.   Ⓒ

   (D) X and Z are connected in parallel.   Ⓓ

9 Which of the following is/are true of ammeters and voltmeters?

    I Ammeters have very low resistance and are connected in series with the component through which they are measuring current.

    II Voltmeters have very high resistance and are connected in parallel with the component across which they are measuring potential difference.

    III An ideal ammeter has infinite resistance and an ideal voltmeter has zero resistance.

(A) I only   Ⓐ

(B) II only   Ⓑ

(C) I and II only   Ⓒ

(D) III only   Ⓓ

Items **10–12** refer to the following diagram.

10 The current through the 1.0 Ω resistor is 2.0 A. What is the potential difference between X and Y?

(A) 4.0 V   Ⓐ

(B) 6.0 V   Ⓑ

(C) 2.0 V   Ⓒ

(D) 10 V   Ⓓ

11 What is the current through the upper branch?

(A) 3.0 A   Ⓐ

(B) 1.5 A   Ⓑ

(C) 6.0 A   Ⓒ

(D) 5.0 A   Ⓓ

12 What is the total resistance between X and Y?

(A) 5.0 Ω   Ⓐ

(B) 2.5 Ω   Ⓑ

(C) 1.2 Ω   Ⓒ

(D) 6.0 Ω   Ⓓ

Items 13–14 refer to the following circuit diagram in which a cell of emf 3.0 V and of negligible internal resistance is connected to resistors X and Y, of resistances $R_X = 6.0$ Ω and $R_Y = 2.0$ Ω, in parallel.

emf 3.0 V

$R_X = 6.0$ Ω

P $R_Y = 2.0$ Ω   Q

13 Which of the following is/are true of the potential difference (pd) across the resistors?

    I The pd across X is 3 times the pd across Y.

    II The pd across X is 3.0 V.

    III The pd between P and Q is 3.0 V.

(A) I only   Ⓐ

(B) I and III only   Ⓑ

(C) II and III only   Ⓒ

(D) III only   Ⓓ

14 Which of the following is/are true of the current through the resistors?

    I The current through X is the same as the current through Y.

    II The current produced by the battery is equal to the sum of the currents in X and Y.

    III The current from the battery is 0.375 A.

(A) I only   Ⓐ

(B) II only   Ⓑ

(C) II and III only   Ⓒ

(D) III only   Ⓓ

Item **15** refers to the following circuit diagram.

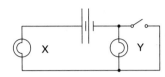

15 Which of the bulbs will glow when the switch is closed?

(A) X only

(B) Y only

(C) X and Y

(D) Neither

Item **16** refers to the following diagram showing the connection between resistors X, Y and Z of resistance $R_X = 2\ \Omega$, $R_Y = 3\ \Omega$ and $R_Z = 1\ \Omega$, respectively.

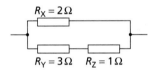

16 Which resistor carries the largest current?

(A) X

(B) Y

(C) Z

(D) They all carry the same current.

Item **17** refers to the following diagram.

$$2\,\Omega \qquad\qquad 4\,\Omega$$

17 The current through the 2 Ω resistor is 10 A. What is the current through the 4 Ω resistor?

(A) 5 A   Ⓐ

(B) 10 A   Ⓑ

(C) 15 A   Ⓒ

(D) 20 A   Ⓓ

18 Which of the following circuits CANNOT be used to determine the resistance of X?

 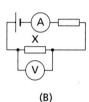 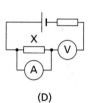

  (A)   (B)   (C)   (D)

Ⓐ

Ⓑ

Ⓒ

Ⓓ

Item **19** refers to the following diagram. The resistors, R, are equal in resistance.

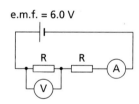

19 The readings on the voltmeter and ammeter are 3.0 V and 2.0 A respectively. What is the resistance of each resistor R?

(A) 6.0 Ω   Ⓐ

(B) 1.5 Ω   Ⓑ

(C) 0.67 Ω   Ⓒ

(D) 3.0 Ω   Ⓓ

20 The following circuit diagrams show the positive pole of each of the measuring instruments used. In which circuit is the connection of the polarity of the measuring instruments correct?

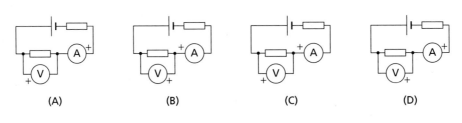

(A)   (B)   (C)   (D)

Ⓐ

Ⓑ

Ⓒ

Ⓓ

21 Which of the following statements are true?

Domestic appliances are connected in parallel because

    I each appliance can then be individually switched on or off without affecting the others.

    II they can then be designed to operate on a standard voltage.

    III if connected in series, the larger the number of appliances, the smaller is the voltage across each of them.

(A) I and II only   Ⓐ

(B) II and III only   Ⓑ

(C) I and III only   Ⓒ

(D) I, II and III   Ⓓ

22 Which of the following is/are true of fuses and circuit breakers?

    I They should be placed in the live or the earth wire of the circuit.

    II They are connected in parallel to the appliance they are to protect.

    III They break the circuit when too large a current flows through it.

(A) I only   Ⓐ

(B) II only   Ⓑ

(C) III only   Ⓒ

(D) I and III only   Ⓓ

Item **23** refers to the following diagram.

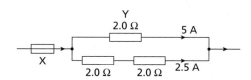

23 Which of the following current ratings of the fuse at X is BEST suited to protect component Y in the circuit? (The currents shown are the normal operational currents of the circuit.)

(A) 2.5 A   (A)

(B) 6 A   (B)

(C) 5 A   (C)

(D) 9 A   (D)

24 Electrical energy consumption of 25 kWh is equivalent to:

(A) 90 MJ   (A)

(B) 90 GJ   (B)

(C) 1.5 MJ   (C)

(D) 25 000 J   (D)

<u>Item 1</u> refers to the following diagrams: three circuit diagrams P, Q and R, and three graphs X, Y and Z of current, *I*, against time, *t*, which are randomly sequenced.

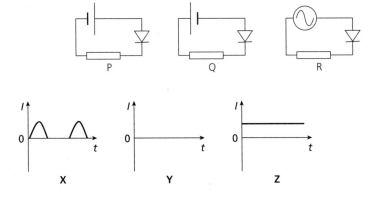

1 Which of the following correctly matches the circuits with their corresponding graphs?

	P	**Q**	**R**	
(A)	X	Z	Y	Ⓐ
(B)	Z	Y	X	Ⓑ
(C)	X	Y	Z	Ⓒ
(D)	Y	X	Z	Ⓓ

2 Which of the following is/are true with respect to the current produced by a battery and that produced by a semiconductor diode which converts ac to dc?

    I The battery produces a constant direct current whereas the diode produces a 'bumpy', continuous alternating current.

    II The current through the diode only flows during one half of each cycle of the alternating emf of the source.

    III Both currents flow in only one direction.

(A) I only   Ⓐ

(B) I and II only   Ⓑ

(C) II and III only   Ⓒ

(D) III only   Ⓓ

3 Rectification is carried out using a

(A) transformer. (A)

(B) generator. (B)

(C) diode. (C)

(D) magnetic relay. (D)

Item **4** refers to the following truth table for four logic gates, whose outputs are W, X, Y and Z.

Inputs		W	X	Y	Z
0	0	1	0	1	0
0	1	1	1	0	0
1	0	1	1	0	0
1	1	0	1	0	1

4 Which of the following correctly matches the logic gates with their outputs?

	AND	OR	NAND	NOR
(A)	Z	X	W	Y
(B)	X	Z	Y	W
(C)	X	W	Z	Y
(D)	W	Y	X	Z

(A)

(B)

(C)

(D)

Item **5** refers to the following digital circuit.

5 If the logic values at the inputs A, B and C are respectively 1, 0 and 1, what are the logic values at D, E and F?

	D	E	F
(A)	1	0	0
(B)	1	1	0
(C)	0	1	1
(D)	0	1	0

(A)

(B)

(C)

(D)

Item **6** refers to the following digital circuit.

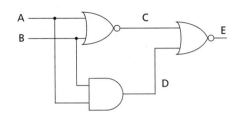

6 If the logic values at the inputs A and B are 1 and 1, what are the logic values at C, D and E?

	C	D	E	
(A)	1	0	0	Ⓐ
(B)	1	1	0	Ⓑ
(C)	0	1	1	Ⓒ
(D)	0	1	0	Ⓓ

D5 Magnetism

1 The pole of a bar magnet X is placed near to one end of another bar Y of unknown material and the bars are observed to attract each other. This reveals that Y is

(A) initially a bar of unmagnetised iron. Ⓐ

(B) a magnet whose end was attracted by an opposite pole of X. Ⓑ

(C) either a bar of unmagnetised, magnetic material, or a magnetised bar whose end was attracted by an opposite pole of X. Ⓒ

(D) a magnet whose end was attracted by a similar pole of X. Ⓓ

Item 2 refers to the following diagram, which shows a bar magnet brought near to an unmagnetised iron bar.

S N		
unmagnetised
iron bar

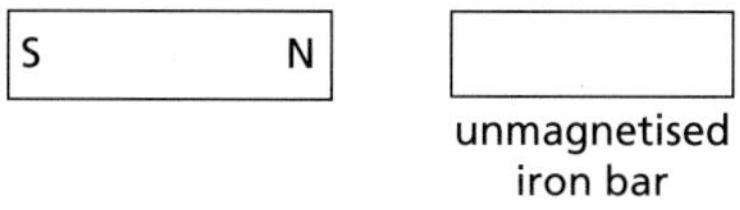

2 How does the presence of the magnet affect the orientation of the atomic dipoles in the iron bar?

(A) Their N poles will face right and their S poles will face left. Ⓐ

(B) Their N poles will face left and their S poles will face right. Ⓑ

(C) Their N poles and S poles will align at right angles to the bar magnet. Ⓒ

(D) The atomic dipoles will become disarranged. Ⓓ

3 A directional compass has a pivoted magnetised needle which tends to settle in a direction

(A) with its N pole pointing approximately to the geographic North pole of the Earth. Ⓐ

(B) with its S pole pointing approximately to the geographic North pole of the Earth. Ⓑ

(C) rotated clockwise with its length at right angles to the Earth's magnetic field. Ⓒ

(D) rotated counterclockwise with its length at right angles to the Earth's magnetic field. Ⓓ

4 Which of the following is/are true of the direction of a magnetic field line?

     I It is the direction in which a free S pole placed in the field would move.

     II It is the direction in which a free N pole placed in the field would move.

     III It is the same at all points within the field, if the field is uniform.

(A) I only Ⓐ

(B) II only Ⓑ

(C) II and III only Ⓒ

(D) III only Ⓓ

<u>Item 5</u> refers to the following diagram, which shows the pattern (by dotted lines) of iron filings due to a magnetic field associated with two bar magnets.

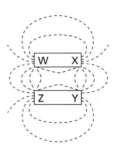

5 If W is a N pole, X, Y and Z are, respectively

(A) S pole, S pole, N pole. Ⓐ

(B) S pole, N pole, S pole. Ⓑ

(C) N pole, S pole, N pole. Ⓒ

(D) N pole, N pole, S pole. Ⓓ

6 Which of the following magnetic field diagrams is correct?

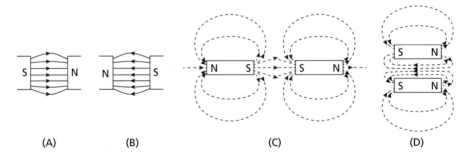

(A)   (B)   (C)   (D)

7 Which of the following magnetic field diagrams is produced when an iron bar, which has NOT previously been magnetised, is placed between two opposite magnetic poles facing each other?

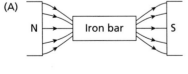

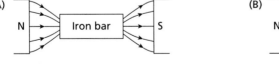

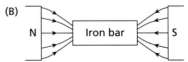

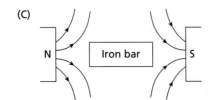

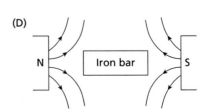

Ⓐ

Ⓑ

Ⓒ

Ⓓ

Item **1** refers to the following diagram showing a current-carrying coil.

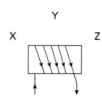

1 Which of the following BEST represents the magnetic field directions at X, Y and Z?

      (A)

      (B)

      (C)

      (D)

Item **2** refers to the following diagram, which shows a short current-carrying coil wrapped through two holes in a piece of card held horizontally.

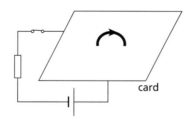

card

2 Which of the following diagrams BEST represents the magnetic field produced, viewed from above?

⊙ = current out of plane of paper
⊗ = current into plane of paper

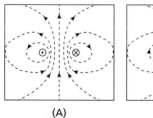

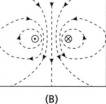

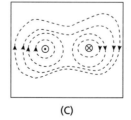

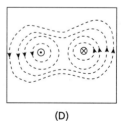

    (A)   (B)   (C)   (D)

3 Which of the following diagrams showing magnetic fields through current-carrying coils is correct?

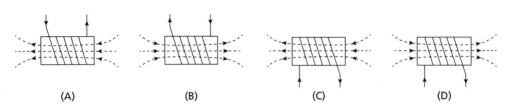

(A)   (B)   (C)   (D)

Ⓐ
Ⓑ
Ⓒ
Ⓓ

4 Which of the following is/are true concerning electromagnets?

   I A soft iron core within the coil greatly increases the strength of the magnetic field.

   II Electromagnets are components in magnetic relays, electric bells and plotting compasses.

   III A steel core within the coil is unsuitable, since it would retain the magnetism when the current is switched off.

(A) I and II only   Ⓐ

(B) II only   Ⓑ

(C) I and III only   Ⓒ

(D) II and III only   Ⓓ

5 Which of the following is NOT true of steel and soft iron?

(A) Soft iron is easy to magnetise.   Ⓐ

(B) Soft iron is easy to demagnetise.   Ⓑ

(C) Electromagnets are wound on steel cores.   Ⓒ

(D) Steel forms good permanent magnets.   Ⓓ

6 Which of the following correctly gives the quantities whose direction is represented by the fingers in Fleming's left-hand rule?

	First finger	Second finger	Thumb	
(A)	Field	Current	Force	Ⓐ
(B)	Current	Field	Force	Ⓑ
(C)	Force	Field	Current	Ⓒ
(D)	Force	Current	Field	Ⓓ

Item 7 refers to the following diagram. X, Y and Z show wires carrying currents through magnetic fields. In X, the current flows into the plane of the diagram, and in Y and Z, it flows in the plane of the diagram in the direction indicated by the arrows.

⊗ = current into plane of paper 　　N ⊗ S 　　　　　　N ↗ S

　　　　　　　　　　　　　　　　　X 　　　　　Y 　　　　　Z

7 Which of the following is true for the direction of the forces created on the wires of diagrams X, Y and Z?

	X	Y	X	
(A)	To top of page	Into page	Out of page	Ⓐ
(B)	To top of page	Into page	Out of page	Ⓑ
(C)	To bottom of page	Into page	Into page	Ⓒ
(D)	To the left	To top of page	To the right	Ⓓ

8 An ideal transformer has 4000 turns on its primary coil and 200 turns on its secondary coil. What voltage is induced across the secondary coil when its primary is connected to a 120 V ac mains?

(A) 6.0 V 　　　　　　　　　　　　　　　　　　　　　　　　　Ⓐ

(B) 12 V 　　　　　　　　　　　　　　　　　　　　　　　　　Ⓑ

(C) 720 V 　　　　　　　　　　　　　　　　　　　　　　　　Ⓒ

(D) 24 V 　　　　　　　　　　　　　　　　　　　　　　　　　Ⓓ

Item **9** refers to the following diagram, which shows an electron beam entering a magnetic field perpendicular to its path.

X = magnetic field into
plane of paper

× × × ×

× × × ×

Electron × × × ×
beam
× × × ×

9 In which direction will the beam deviate?

(A) To the top of the page   (A)

(B) To the bottom of the page   (B)

(C) Out of the page   (C)

(D) Into the page   (D)

Item **10** refers to the following diagram.

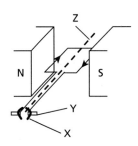

10 The type of device and the names of its parts X, Y and Z could be

	Device	X	Y	Z	
(A)	ac generator	Graphite brush	Coil	Bearing	(A)
(B)	dc motor	Slip rings	Carbon brush	Axle	(B)
(C)	dc motor	Commutator	Graphite brush	Axle	(C)
(D)	ac generator	Armature	Commutator	Pivot	(D)

11 Which of the following does NOT increase the force on the coil of a dc electric motor?

(A) An increase in current in coil. ⒜

(B) An increase in number of turns of coil. ⒝

(C) An increase in resistance of coil. ⒞

(D) An increase in strength of magnet. ⒟

12 In which of the following cases is an emf NOT induced?

(A) A magnet being pushed into a coil of conducting wire. ⒜

(B) A metal rod moving in random directions within a magnetic field. ⒝

(C) A magnet at rest in a coil of conducting wire. ⒞

(D) A coil carrying an alternating current placed next to another conducting coil. ⒟

13 Which of the following is/are true of induced currents?

    I The induced current always opposes the motion creating it.

    II Induced currents are proportional to the relative motion at which a conductor cuts through magnetic flux.

    III Once a conductor is in a magnetic field, it will induce a current.

(A) I and II only ⒜

(B) II only ⒝

(C) I and III only ⒞

(D) II and III only ⒟

14 Which of the following is/are true of the size of the induced emf when a magnet is pushed into a conducting coil?

    I It increases if the magnet is moved faster.

    II It decreases if there are fewer turns of coil.

    III It increases if a stronger magnet is used.

(A) I only ⒜

(B) I and II only ⒝

(C) II and III only ⒞

(D) I, II and III ⒟

15 The following diagrams show a magnet being pushed into and pulled from a coil connected to a centre-zero galvanometer. Which diagram correctly shows the induced polarity of the coil and the direction of induced current within it?

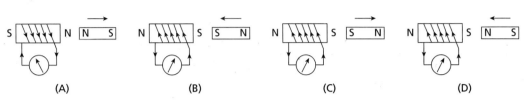

(A)   (B)   (C)   (D)

     Ⓐ
     Ⓑ
     Ⓒ
     Ⓓ

16 The maximum emf induced by the rotating coil of an ac generator occurs as it cuts through the magnetic field lines at an angle of

(A) $30°$ Ⓐ

(B) $60°$ Ⓑ

(C) $90°$ Ⓒ

(D) $120°$ Ⓓ

17 Which of the following is/are true of a transformer?

     I It transforms ac to dc.

     II If it changes a current from 5 A to 10 A, it is a step-up transformer.

     III It takes ac at its input and produces ac at its output.

(A) I only   Ⓐ

(B) II only   Ⓑ

(C) II and III only   Ⓒ

(D) III only   Ⓓ

18 Which of the following is NOT true of a transformer?

(A) It has a laminated core to reduce eddy currents and therefore lessens the amount of thermal energy produced.

(A)

(B) A current does not flow from the primary coil to the secondary coil.

(B)

(C) If the number of turns on the secondary coil is twice that on the primary coil, then for an ideal transformer, the current induced in the secondary coil is also twice the current in the primary coil.

(C)

(D) If the voltage across the secondary coil is twice that across the primary coil, then for an ideal transformer, the current flowing in the secondary coil will be half that flowing in the primary coil.

(D)

19 The primary coil of an ideal transformer is plugged into a 120 V ac supply and correctly operates a 6.0 V, 5.0 A device. What is the current in the primary coil?

(A) 0.25 A

(A)

(B) 24 A

(B)

(C) 100 A

(C)

(D) 4.0 A

(D)

20 Which of the following is NOT true concerning the transmission of electricity as alternating current from the production plant to the consumer?

(A) Unlike dc, the current can be reduced to a very low value by means of a transformer, resulting in less energy being wasted as heat through the transmission lines.

(A)

(B) Alternating current can easily be reduced to low values by a transformer and therefore the power lines can be made with thinner, less costly material.

(B)

(C) The consumer can operate machinery and devices of several different voltage requirements with the use of a transformer to step up or step down the received voltage.

(C)

(D) The transmission current is increased if the transmission voltage is increased.

(D)

Section E: The Physics of the Atom
E1 Models and structure of the atom

1 Which scientist was responsible for the discovery of the neutron, and which scientist predicted the existence of electron shells around the atomic nucleus?

	Discovery of neutron	Prediction of electron shells	
(A)	Bohr	Rutherford	Ⓐ
(B)	Chadwick	Bohr	Ⓑ
(C)	Thomson	Curie	Ⓒ
(D)	Becquerel	Rutherford	Ⓓ

2 Which scientist was responsible for the discovery of radium, and which scientist suggested the 'plum pudding' concept of the atom?

	Discovery of radium	Suggestion of 'plum pudding' concept	
(A)	Newton	Rutherford	Ⓐ
(B)	Einstein	Bohr	Ⓑ
(C)	Curie	Thomson	Ⓒ
(D)	Becquerel	Rutherford	Ⓓ

3 Which of the following is/are true of the Geiger–Marsden experiment?

  I Alpha particles were shot through gold foil in an evacuated chamber and it was noticed that most of them were deflected strongly, but a few passed through without deviation.

  II It was done under the direction of Ernest Rutherford.

  III It revealed that the atom was mainly empty space but contained a small, concentrated, positively charged nucleus.

(A) I only   Ⓐ

(B) I and II only   Ⓑ

(C) II and III only   Ⓒ

(D) III only   Ⓓ

4 An atomic nuclide of nickel is represented as $^{62}_{28}N$. Which of the following is/are true of an atom of this nickel?

    I Its nucleon number is 28.

    II It has an atomic number of 62 and a mass number of 28.

    III The number of protons in the nucleus of its atom is 28.

    IV The number of electrons in a neutral atom of the nuclide is 28.

(A) I and III only   Ⓐ

(B) II and III only   Ⓑ

(C) III only   Ⓒ

(D) III and IV only   Ⓓ

5 Which of the following is/are true of isotopes of the same element?

    I They have the same mass number.

    II They have the same number of protons in their atomic nucleus.

    III A possible isotope of $^{56}_{26}Fe$ is $^{56}_{27}Fe$.

(A) I only   Ⓐ

(B) II only   Ⓑ

(C) I and III only   Ⓒ

(D) II and III only   Ⓓ

1 Which scientist established the link between mass and energy, $E = mc^2$, and which scientist concluded that radioactivity is an 'atomic phenomenon' because the intensity of its emissions is independent of environmental conditions?

	$E = mc^2$	Radioactivity as an atomic phenomenon	
(A)	Newton	Rutherford	Ⓐ
(B)	Einstein	Curie	Ⓑ
(C)	Curie	Thomson	Ⓒ
(D)	Becquerel	Rutherford	Ⓓ

2 Which of the following statements about alpha and beta particles is INCORRECT?

(A) The alpha particle has a relative charge of +2. Ⓐ

(B) The alpha particle has a mass relative to the proton of 4. Ⓑ

(C) The beta particle has a mass relative to the proton of about 1840. Ⓒ

(D) The alpha particle has twice the charge of a beta particle (electron), but it is opposite in sign. Ⓓ

3 W, X, Y and Z are four radioactive emissions. W is electromagnetic in nature; X passes through paper but is stopped by about 4 mm of aluminium; Y can penetrate several cm of lead; Z is stopped by a thin sheet of paper. What are the types of emissions?

	W	X	Y	Z	
(A)	Alpha	Gamma	Beta	Alpha	Ⓐ
(B)	Gamma	Beta	Gamma	Alpha	Ⓑ
(C)	Beta	Gamma	Beta	Alpha	Ⓒ
(D)	Gamma	Beta	Alpha	Gamma	Ⓓ

<u>Item 4</u> refers to the following diagram, which shows three different radioactive emissions passing through a magnetic field and being detected by detectors P, Q and R.

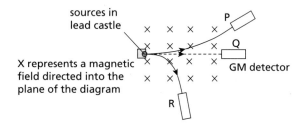

4 The emissions detected by the detectors are

	P	**Q**	**R**	
(A)	α	β	γ	Ⓐ
(B)	β	α	γ	Ⓑ
(C)	α	γ	β	Ⓒ
(D)	β	γ	α	Ⓓ

<u>Item 5</u> refers to the following diagram, which shows three different radioactive emissions passing through an electric field and being detected by detectors P, Q and R.

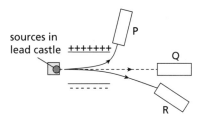

5 The emissions detected by the detectors are

	P	**Q**	**R**	
(A)	α	β	γ	Ⓐ
(B)	β	α	γ	Ⓑ
(C)	α	γ	β	Ⓒ
(D)	β	γ	α	Ⓓ

Item **6** refers to the following diagram, which shows tracks produced in a cloud chamber by three different radioactive emissions.

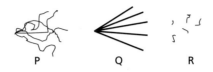

6 The emissions are

	P	Q	R	
(A)	α	β	γ	Ⓐ
(B)	β	α	γ	Ⓑ
(C)	α	γ	β	Ⓒ
(D)	β	γ	α	Ⓓ

7 The decay of U-238 is as follows: $^{238}_{92}U \rightarrow {}^{w}_{x}\alpha + {}^{y}_{z}Th$. The values of w, x, y and z are

	w	x	y	z	
(A)	4	2	90	234	Ⓐ
(B)	0	−1	90	234	Ⓑ
(C)	2	4	234	90	Ⓒ
(D)	4	2	234	90	Ⓓ

8 The decay of Th-234 is as follows: $^{234}_{w}Th \rightarrow {}^{x}_{y}\beta + {}^{z}_{91}Pa$. The values of w, x, y and z are

	w	x	y	z	
(A)	90	0	−1	234	Ⓐ
(B)	90	−1	0	234	Ⓑ
(C)	92	0	−1	235	Ⓒ
(D)	89	−1	0	233	Ⓓ

9 Which of the following is NOT true of natural radioactivity?

(A) It is due to nuclear instability. ⒶⒶ

(B) It is dependent on physical and chemical conditions. Ⓑ

(C) It is a random process. Ⓒ

(D) It converts matter to energy as it occurs. Ⓓ

10 Which TWO of the following are true of the half-life of a radioisotope?

    I It is half the time for a sample of it to decay completely.

    II It is half the time for its activity to diminish to zero.

    III It is the time for its mass to fall to half its value.

    IV It is the time for half of its particles to decay radioactively.

(A) I and II only Ⓐ

(B) I and III only Ⓑ

(C) II and IV only Ⓒ

(D) III and IV only Ⓓ

<u>Item **11**</u> refers to the following graph showing the decay of a radioisotope.

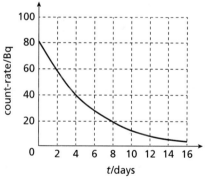

11 The half-life of the radioisotope is

(A) 2 days Ⓐ

(B) 4 days Ⓑ

(C) 6 days Ⓒ

(D) 8 days Ⓓ

12 The activity of a radioisotope falls to 12.5% of its value in 24 days. What is its half-life?

(A) 4 days   Ⓐ

(B) 6 days   Ⓑ

(C) 8 days   Ⓒ

(D) 12 days   Ⓓ

13 A radioisotope with a half-life of 5700 years decays for a period of 17 100 years. If the sample initially contained 8×10^{12} particles, the number of particles remaining after this time is

(A) 1×10^{12} Ⓐ

(B) 2×10^{12} Ⓑ

(C) 4×10^{12} Ⓒ

(D) 6×10^{12} Ⓓ

14 The Sun emits energy at 3.6×10^{23} per second. Given that the speed of light is 3.0×10^{8} m s^{-1}, what mass does the Sun lose every second?

(A) 2.0×10^{5} kg

(B) 1.2×10^{15} kg

(C) 4.0×10^{6} kg

(D) 6.0×10^{4} kg